GREAT
AMERICAN
QUILTS
1992

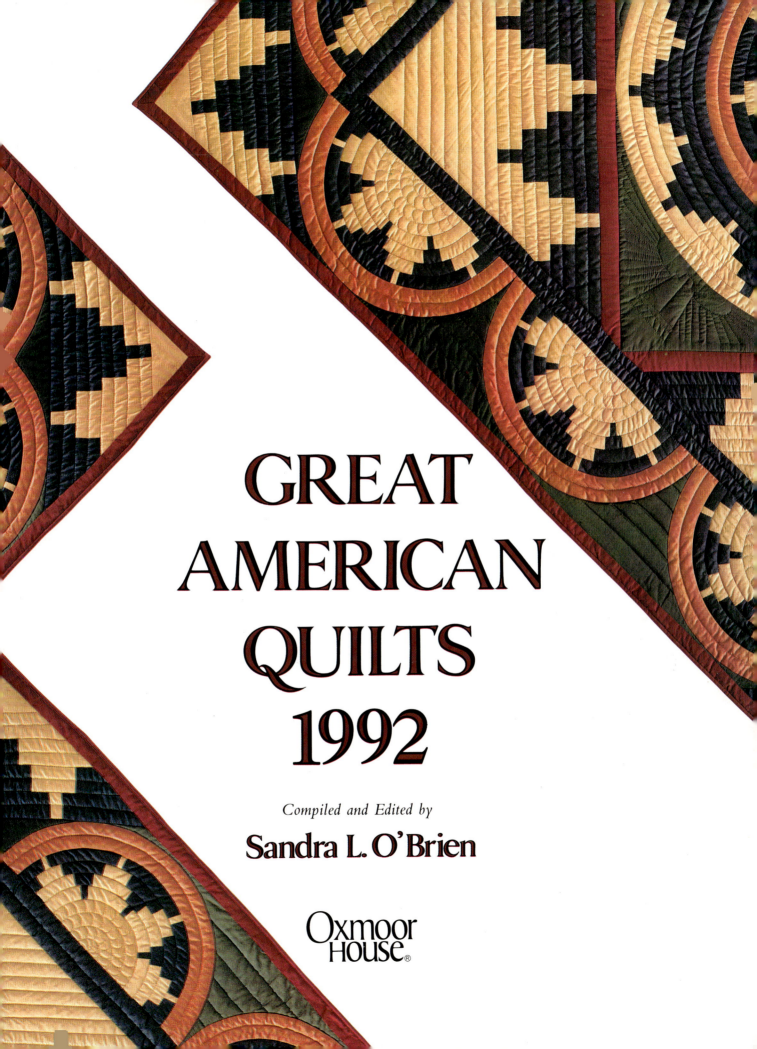

GREAT AMERICAN QUILTS 1992

Compiled and Edited by

Sandra L. O'Brien

Oxmoor House®

Library of Congress Catalog Number: 86-62283
ISBN: 0-8487-1065-7
ISSN: 0890-8222
Manufactured in the United States of America
First Printing 1991

Executive Editor: Nancy J. Fitzpatrick
Director of Manufacturing: Jerry Higdon
Art Director: Bob Nance
Copy Chief: Mary Jean Haddin

Great American Quilts 1992

Editor: Sandra L. O'Brien
Editorial Assistant: Catherine S. Corbett
Designer: Melinda P. Goode
Senior Photographer: John O'Hagan
Patterns and Illustrations: Karen L. Tindall, Larry Hunter
Assistant Copy Editor: Susan Smith Cheatham
Production Manager: Rick Litton
Associate Production Manager: Theresa L. Beste
Production Assistant: Pam Bullock

CONTENTS

EDITOR'S NOTE

Wooden basket, fruit basket, flower basket, picnic basket, bread basket! Both a container and a decorative item, the basket in all its various forms has been with us for centuries. Therefore, it is no wonder that the basket design appears repeatedly in some of our earliest quilts. No wonder, also, that it remains a popular design among quilters today.

Our opening chapter, "The Basket Patch," is an assortment of quilts with pieced or appliquéd basket patterns. Joyce Stewart of Rexburg, Idaho, opens this chapter with her contemporary interpretation of Marie Webster's French Basket pattern. Sara Ann McLennand of Wellington, Florida, introduces you to Indian flat basket design with her *Duck Island Basket* quilt. (It also graces our cover.) This most ambitious project requires patience to piece all the curves, but you will know it was worth the effort when you see the results.

A willingness to try new and different techniques and products is a distinction of most quilters' personalities. If it were not so, quilt exhibits, quilt shops, and quilt publications would not be so popular. Among the quilters featured in our "Quilts Across America" chapter are two who use a mixed-media approach to quiltmaking. Kim Brooks of Lewiston, Idaho, teaches you the process for making brush batik and using the designs formed by waxing and dyeing as appliqué figures, similar to the way printed fabric is used

for *broderie perse*. And Linda Lewis of Kailua, Hawaii, shows you how to embellish your fabrics with paint for a quick quilted wall hanging and a bunch of zippy patchwork ornaments.

Jennifer Rozens of Detroit introduces you to a trio of her ancestors in our "Traditions in Quilting" chapter. They completed a set of patchwork blocks in the late 1800s. And you guessed it— Jennifer's first quilt, *Evening Star*, is made from those same blocks. Her story speaks to all quilters about the value of saving fabric scraps and leftover blocks.

Our "Bee Quilters" chapter has an international flavor this year because of the Rather Bees in Grand Island, Nebraska. Rather Bee member Rita Hays initiated a quiltmaking project among the members of three guilds—one from the United States, one from Australia, and one from England. Twenty-one quilts have been made from their overseas swapping of quilt blocks and fabrics, and their *International Ohio Star* is an example of their worldly workmanship.

A festival of spectacular scenery and design in fabric form awaits you in our "Designer Gallery." Hours of hard work and diligence went into the making of these complex quilts. Honor them with your time and linger over the artistic talents displayed by these quilters.

Last but not least, before proceeding read our Preliminary Instructions below. We also suggest familiarizing yourself with quiltmaking instructions before trying to make any quilt. Being aware of the number of borders and border widths is essential before cutting fabrics.

Preliminary Instructions

All pattern pieces include ¼-inch seam allowance. All measurements for pieces, sashing, and border strips are given including seam allowances, unless

otherwise noted. Some oversize pieces are placed on a grid, with scale information noted.

Fabric requirements are based on 44/45-inch fabric with trimmed selvages, and requirements for backing on bed quilts are based on a three-panel backing. *Generous allowances are given for fabric requirements to account for fabric shrinkage and individual differences in cutting.* Fabric requirements are given for one-piece borders. We suggest that you wash, dry, and press fabrics before using. Finished quilt size is the size of the quilt before quilting.

How Can You Be Featured in *Great American Quilts*?

Every week we receive letters from quilters across the country, wanting to know how they can submit a quilt for publication in *Great American Quilts*. Well, it's easy! Just write to the editor of *Great American Quilts* at Oxmoor House, Inc., 2100 Lakeshore Drive, Birmingham, AL 35209. Include your name and address, and we'll send the application forms for you or your guild, or both.

THE
BASKET
PATCH

Joyce Winterton Stewart

Rexburg, Idaho

It took strip piecing to sell Joyce on quiltmaking. "I thought patch-work piecing was slow and time-consuming when I first tried quilt-making in 1981," says Joyce. "After that, I didn't want to make another one, until I enrolled in a strip-piecing class and learned that quiltmaking could be fun and fast."

Once Joyce got rolling (or should we say her rotary cutter got rolling!), a succession of awards followed. Her quilts were featured in *Quilt World Omnibook* in 1984, *Quilt Art '86* and *'90* engagement calendars, *Quilter's Newsletter*, and *American Quilter*. She won an award for excellence in quilting, first place ribbons, best of show, and one of her quilts was selected as the Idaho winner in the Great American Quilt contest. The list goes on and on. Her sampler quilt, *Crossing Over Time*, was selected for Oxmoor House's *1991 Sampler Quilt Calendar*.

Wicker Baskets
1987

A mixture of the old with the new is the best way to describe Joyce's vibrant *Wicker Baskets*. The quilt is an interpretation of a traditional pattern, French Basket, designed by Marie Webster in 1915 for *The Ladies' Home Journal*. (The pattern is also known as The Ivory Basket, the name given it by Mrs. Scioto I. Danner, whose quilt catalogs were famous in the 1930s.)

For a lesson in how you can add a personal touch to or simplify a traditional pattern, study the origi-nal French Basket design, found on page 79 of Woodard and Green-stein's *Twentieth Century Quilts 1900-1950*. Then compare the French Basket pattern to Joyce's pattern. Her contemporary setting for these baskets can inspire us all to try setting traditional patterns in new ways.

This wall hanging has a sampling of several techniques to challenge your quilting skills. There's plenty of layer-appliquéing, a touch of re-verse appliqué, and an abundance of strip piecing.

Wicker Baskets

Finished Quilt Size
43″ x 43″

Number of Blocks and Finished Size
4 Basket blocks—10½″ x 10½″
5 Irish Chain blocks—10½″ x 10½″

Fabric Requirements
Brown print   —1⅓ yd.
Red print   —¼ yd.
Red   —1½ yd.
Cream   —1½ yd.
Green   —1½ yd.
Dk. green   —1½ yd.
Green for bias
  binding   —1 yd.
Backing   —1½ yd.

Other Materials
Posterboard

Number to Cut★
Template A   —4 brown print
Template B   —16 red
                8 red print
Template C   —24 red
Template D   —4 red
                24 red print
Template E   —4 green
Template E★★   —4 green
Template F   —4 green
Template F★★   —4 green
Template G   —4 green
Template G★★   —4 green
Template H   —4 green
Template H★★   —4 green

★See table on page 14 for strip dimensions before cutting fabric.
★★Flip or turn over template if fabric is one-sided.

Quilt Top Assembly
1. Cut four 11½″ squares from cream. Finger-crease squares in half twice to find the center. Cut bias strips, ¾″ wide, from brown print for basket handles. Center basket handles and basket (A) on block. (Cut slits for reverse appliqué in basket before pinning to block.)

Handles are made using 2 strips of bias. Weave the strips over and under, pinning or basting them in place as needed. Appliqué handles to block, beginning with the inner curves.

Reverse-appliqué slits in basket and appliqué basket to block. Arrange remaining pieces on block, as shown in Basket Placement Diagram. Cut bias strips, ¾″ wide,

from green for stems. Layer-appliqué pieces in the numerical order shown in parentheses in Basket Placement Diagram.

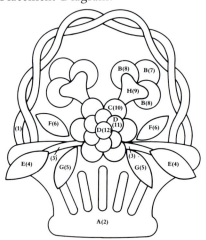

Basket Placement Diagram

Joyce used the posterboard method to appliqué perfect circles. Cut circles B, C, and D without seam allowance from posterboard. Center posterboard circle on fabric circle. Take gathering stitches in

seam allowance and pull tight to secure fabric around the posterboard circle and to create a smooth edge for appliquéing. Appliqué circle to block with posterboard inside. Cut fabric from behind circle and remove posterboard.

After each block is appliquéd, trim all blocks to 11″ x 11″. Cut out fabric from behind pieces, leaving ¼″ seam allowance.

2. Cut strips as listed in table on page 14.

Join strips lengthwise to make Panels 1 through 6, as shown in Chart of Strip-Pieced Panels. Cut across seam lines at 2″ intervals and make number of segments indicated in chart for each panel.

In addition, cut strips, 2″ wide, from cream and make 6 rectangles, 2″ x 5″, and 10 rectangles, 2″ x 8″. (Four 2″ x 8″ rectangles will be used in center border block.)

Join rectangles and segments from Panels 1, 2, 3, and 5 to make Irish Chain Block 1, as shown in Irish Chain Block 1 Piecing Diagrams.

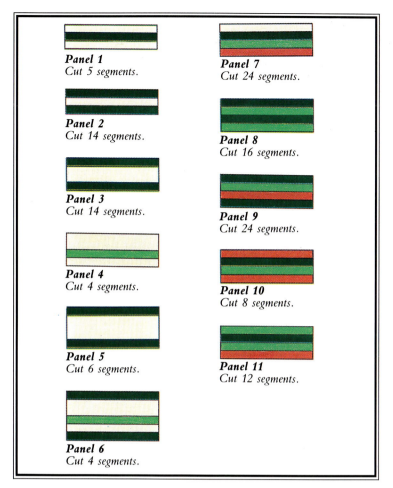

Panel 1
Cut 5 segments.

Panel 2
Cut 14 segments.

Panel 3
Cut 14 segments.

Panel 4
Cut 4 segments.

Panel 5
Cut 6 segments.

Panel 6
Cut 4 segments.

Panel 7
Cut 24 segments.

Panel 8
Cut 16 segments.

Panel 9
Cut 24 segments.

Panel 10
Cut 8 segments.

Panel 11
Cut 12 segments.

Chart of Strip Pieced Panels

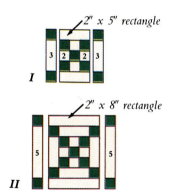

2″ x 5″ rectangle

I

2″ x 8″ rectangle

II

Irish Chain Block 1 Piecing Diagrams

Join rectangles and segments from Panels 1 through 6 to make 4 Irish Chain Block 2s, as shown in Irish Chain Block 2 Piecing Diagram. (Arrow indicates top of block.)

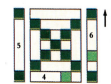

Irish Chain Block 2 Piecing Diagram
Make 4.

3. Alternate Wicker Basket blocks with Irish Chain blocks to make 3 rows of 3 blocks each, as shown in Setting Diagram. Pay close attention to directional arrows for proper block placement. Join blocks at sides to form rows. Join rows.

CC ↑	BB ↓	CBB ↓	BBR ↓	CB ←
BBR →	IC2 ↓	WB	IC2 ←	BB
CBB →	WB	IC1 ↑	WB	CBB ←
BB →	IC2	WB ↑	IC2 ↑	BBR ←
CB →	BBR ↑	CBB ↑	BB ↑	CB ↑

Setting Diagram

IC1 = Irish Chain Block 1
IC2 = Irish Chain Block 2
WB = Wicker Basket Block
BB = Border Block
BBR = Border Block, Reversed
CBB = Center Border Block
CB = Corner Block

Arrows indicate top of blocks.

4. Join remaining strips lengthwise to make Panels 7 through 11. Cut across seam lines at 2″ intervals and make number of segments indicated.

5. Join segments from Panels 7 through 10 to make border blocks, as shown in Border Block Piecing Diagram. Make number indicated.

7 8 7 9 7 8 10

Border Block Piecing Diagram
Make 4 as shown. Make 4 in reverse order.

6. Cut 1 strip each from red and green, 2″ wide. Cut across strips at 2″ intervals and make 4 red squares and 8 green squares. Join a green square to each end of Panel 2 segment, as shown in Center Border Block Piecing Diagram I. Join a red square to one end of Panel 11 segment, as shown.

2″ x 8″ rectangle

+

Panel 3 segment

+

Panel 2 segment + 2 green squares

+

Panel 11 segment + red square

Center Border Block Piecing Diagram I

Join cream rectangle (2″ x 8″) and segments, as shown in Center Border Block Piecing Diagram I. Join segments from Panel 9 to opposite sides of block, as shown in Center Border Block Piecing Diagram II. Make 4 blocks.

9   9

Center Border Block Piecing Diagram II
Make 4.

7. Join segments from Panels 9 and 11, as shown in Corner Block Piecing Diagram. Make 4 corner blocks.

9 11 11 9

Corner Block Piecing Diagram
Make 4.

8. Place a center border block between border blocks and join at sides. (See Setting Diagram for proper positioning of blocks.) Make 4. Join 2 to opposite sides of quilt.

Join corner blocks to opposite ends of remaining borders, noting proper position before joining. Join to quilt. (For an explanation of half squares on quilt edges, see Finished Edges.)

Quilting

Outline-quilt outside all appliquéd pieces. A ¼" cross-hatching pattern is quilted between basket handles and flowers. Quilt parallel lines to frame each basket, as shown in quilt photograph. Borders are quilted with a 1" cross-hatching pattern.

Finished Edges

To give the look of half squares on the border's outside edge, Joyce trimmed ½" off the edge of her quilt. Bind quilt with green fabric, leaving a ½"-wide binding.

Size of Strips and Number to Cut for Strip-Pieced Panels

Fabric	Dimensions*	Total Number to Cut	Panel/s
Cream	2" x 10"	2	4, 6
	2" x 12"	2	1
	2" x 30"	1	2
	2" x 50"	1	7
	5" x 10"	2	4, 6
	5" x 30"	1	3
	8" x 14"	1	5
Green	2" x 10"	2	4, 6
	2" x 18"	1	10
	2" x 26"	2	11
	2" x 34"	2	8
	2" x 50"	2	7, 9
Dark Green	2" x 10"	2	6
	2" x 12"	1	1
	2" x 14"	2	5
	2" x 18"	1	10
	2" x 26"	1	11
	2" x 30"	4	2, 3
	2" x 34"	2	8
	2" x 50"	3	7, 9
Red	2" x 18"	2	10
	2" x 26"	1	11
	2" x 50"	2	7, 9

*Measurements are padded to allow for cutting errors.

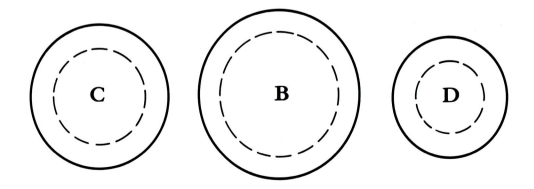

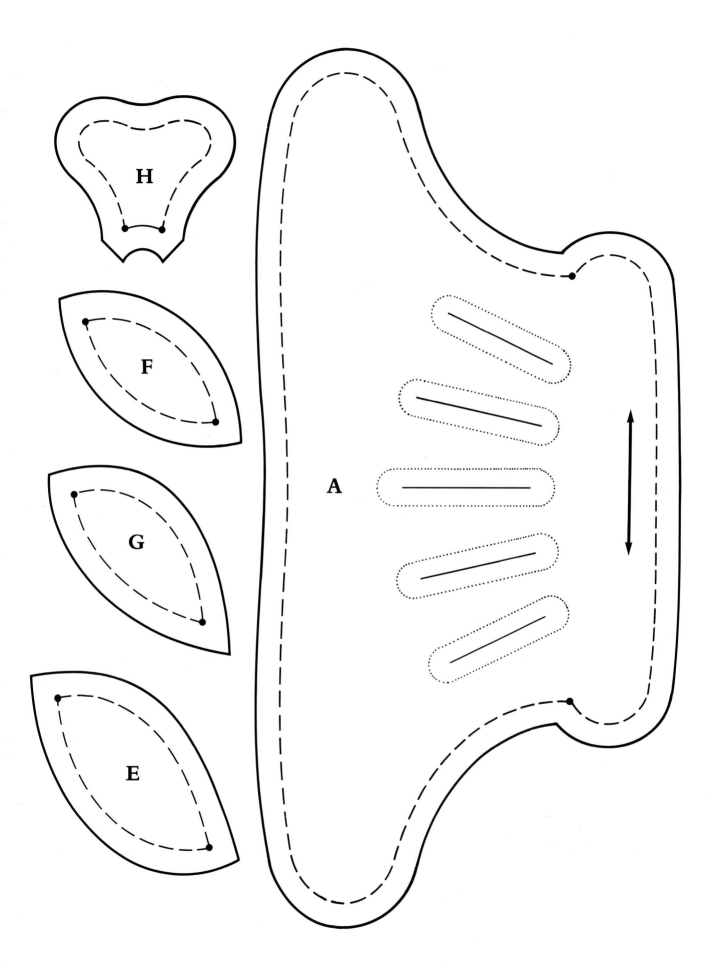

Mary Lou Thayer

South Easton, Massachusetts

"Translating the quilt in my mind to fabric," says Mary Lou, "is the most satisfying part of quiltmaking for me." Mary Lou grew up in an atmosphere that encouraged sewing, painting, and most kinds of handwork, but not quilting. It was not until 1981, when a friend persuaded her to attend a quiltmaking class, that she was introduced to quilting. It was love at first sight! Eleven years later, she has completed over 30 quilts.

Mary Lou is a member of the Rhododendron Needlers Quilt Guild in Norwood, Massachusetts, and her quilting activities have the year-round support of her family. "Both of my daughters enjoy making their own quilts, too," says Mary Lou, "and my husband and son are very proud when they see our work hanging in shows."

Amish Basket Medallion
1990

Quilted hearts and pieced baskets combine to make this elegant quilt. Originally, Mary Lou had planned to appliqué flowers around the basket medallion. "But when the quilt was pieced," she says, "I found that I preferred it without the flowers, and that a feathered heart fit perfectly in the space." A flange of rose chintz accents the pieced center like a mat on a framed picture.

Amish Basket Medallion won a blue ribbon and Viewer's Choice Award at the Perinton Quilt Show, Perinton, New York, in March 1990.

Amish Basket Medallion

Finished Quilt Size
69" x 83"

Number of Blocks and Finished Size
16 Basket blocks—10" x 10"

Fabric Requirements

Cranberry	—½ yd.
Cranberry print	—½ yd.
Rose chintz	—½ yd.
Navy	—2½ yd.
Blue print	—1¾ yd.
White	—2⅝ yd.
Navy for bias binding	—1 yd.
Backing	—4½ yd.

Number to Cut

Template A	—20 cranberry
	4 navy★
	16 blue print
	36 white
Template B	—24 white
Template C	—24 rose chintz★
	56 cranberry print
	32 navy★
	152 blue print
	192 white
Template D	—32 white
Template E	—14 blue print
Template F	—4 blue print
10½" square	—12 white

★See steps 4 and 5 before cutting fabrics.

Quilt Top Assembly

1. Join pieces A through C to make blocks for medallion, as shown in Medallion Piecing Diagrams. Make 4.

I

II

Medallion Piecing Diagrams

2. Join pieces A through D to make Basket block, as shown in photograph and Basket Piecing Diagrams. Make 14 blocks with cranberry print triangles (C) (shown in photograph) and 2 blocks with rose chintz triangles (C).

I

II

Basket Piecing Diagrams

3. Arrange medallion blocks, Basket blocks, 10½" squares, and triangles E and F in diagonal rows and corner sections, as shown in

Setting Diagram and quilt photograph, and join. Join rows and corner sections to complete quilt center.

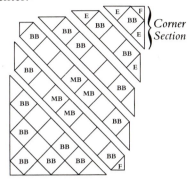

BB = Basket Block
MB = Medallion Block

Setting Diagram

4. For flange between quilt center and border, cut strips, 1″ wide, from rose chintz the length and width of the quilt. Mary Lou recommends cutting these strips across the grain; therefore, strips will need to be pieced. Leave a generous seam allowance at ends of strips for ease in handling when flanges are mitered. Fold strips in half lengthwise and press. Match raw edges of flange to quilt and join to quilt, keeping folded edge of flange free of seam. Leave corners unstitched. The flanges will be sewn into the mitering seam of the border.
5. Cut 4 borders, 6¾″ wide, from navy. Join to quilt and miter corners. Include flanges in the mitering seam, as mentioned in step 4.

Quilting
Outline-quilt outside seams of medallion and Basket block pieces. Use quilting patterns for the center of the medallion and triangles (E and F). Feathered hearts are quilted in the large white areas, as shown in quilt photograph. Feather quilting also flows along the navy border.

Finished Edges
Bind with navy fabric.

Quilting Pattern for Center of Medallion

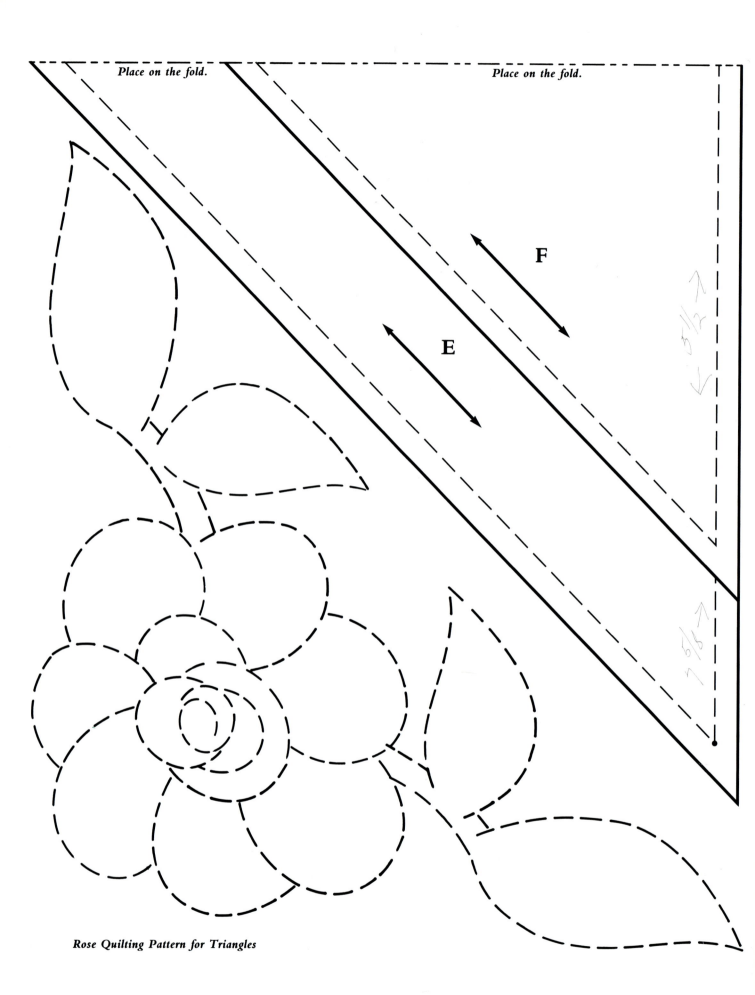

F

E

Rose Quilting Pattern for Triangles

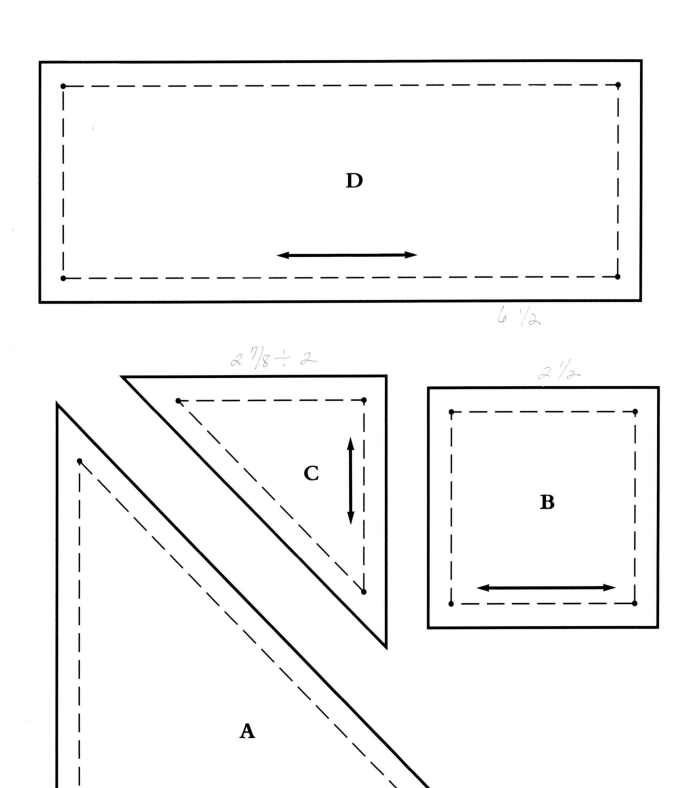

D

$6\frac{1}{2}$

$2\frac{7}{8} \div 2$

C

$2\frac{1}{2}$

B

A

$4\frac{7}{8}$ sq $\div 2$

Wilma L. Waxler

Malta, Ohio

Whenever she has the opportunity, Wilma is busy at work on a quilt. "I'm a person who has to keep my fingers busy," she says. "I always have several projects started, so I can pick one up at any time."

Wilma began sewing when she was 10 years old and hasn't stopped yet. She completed two quilts when she was a teenager and has worked as a dressmaker most of her life. After her children were grown and gone, she had more time to work on quilts. Her quilts are hand-pieced, and she especially favors the traditional patterns. "I love the old quilts that are well made," says Wilma, "so I try to attend as many quilt shows as I can to see them."

Flower Basket
1983

This quilt is very special to Wilma because it contains the floral print fabric from a housecoat that her mother made for her. "I decided to use the fabric in a quilt," says Wilma, "because that way I could always enjoy it." In addition, the Flower Basket pattern was one that her mother had in her collection.

The quilt is large enough to use on a queen-size bed. Extensive quilting, particularly on the borders, is indicative of Wilma's thoroughness in quiltmaking, even on such a large project.

Flower Basket

Finished Quilt Size
95" x 118"

Number of Blocks and Finished Size
63 blocks—8" x 8"

Fabric Requirements
Muslin	—3½ yd.
Lavender	—3½ yd.
Floral print	—3¼ yd.
Green	—6 yd.
Green for bias binding	—1¼ yd.
Backing	—10¼ yd.

Number to Cut
Template A	—63 lavender★
Template B	—126 muslin
Template C	—126 lavender★
Template D	—63 muslin
Template E	—126 floral print★
	126 green★
Template F	—252 muslin
Template G	—63 muslin
Template H	—28 green★
Template I	—4 green★
8½" squares	—48 green★

★See steps 3, 4, and 5 before cutting fabrics.

Quilt Top Assembly
1. Join pieces A through G for basket block, as shown in Block Piecing Diagram. Center 2 floral print diamonds (E) between green diamonds (E), as shown. Join pieces to make 2 large pieced triangles. Join triangles with a long center seam. Make 63 blocks.

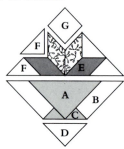

Block Piecing Diagram

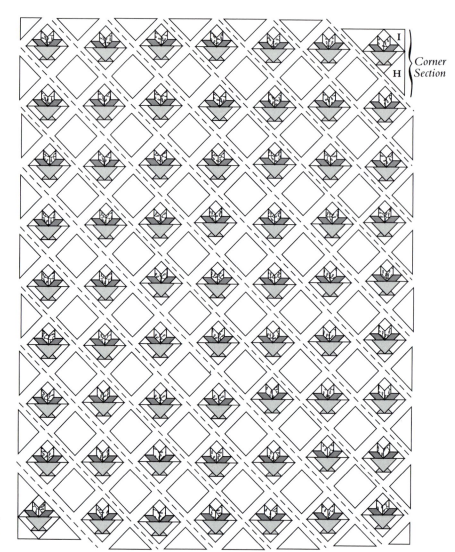

Setting Diagram

2. Arrange basket blocks, 8½" squares, and triangles (H, I) in diagonal rows and corner sections, as shown in Setting Diagram, and join. Join rows and corner sections.
3. Cut 4 borders, 1½" wide, from lavender. Join to quilt and miter corners.
4. Cut 4 borders, 3" wide, from floral print. Join to quilt and miter corners.
5. Cut 4 borders, 5" wide, from green. Join to quilt and miter corners.

Quilting
Outline-quilt ¼" inside seam lines of all pieces in basket blocks.

A feathered wreath is quilted in each 8½" square, and half-wreaths are quilted in each triangle H. Quilt borders with a 1¼" diagonal cross-hatching pattern.

Finished Edges
Bind with green fabric.

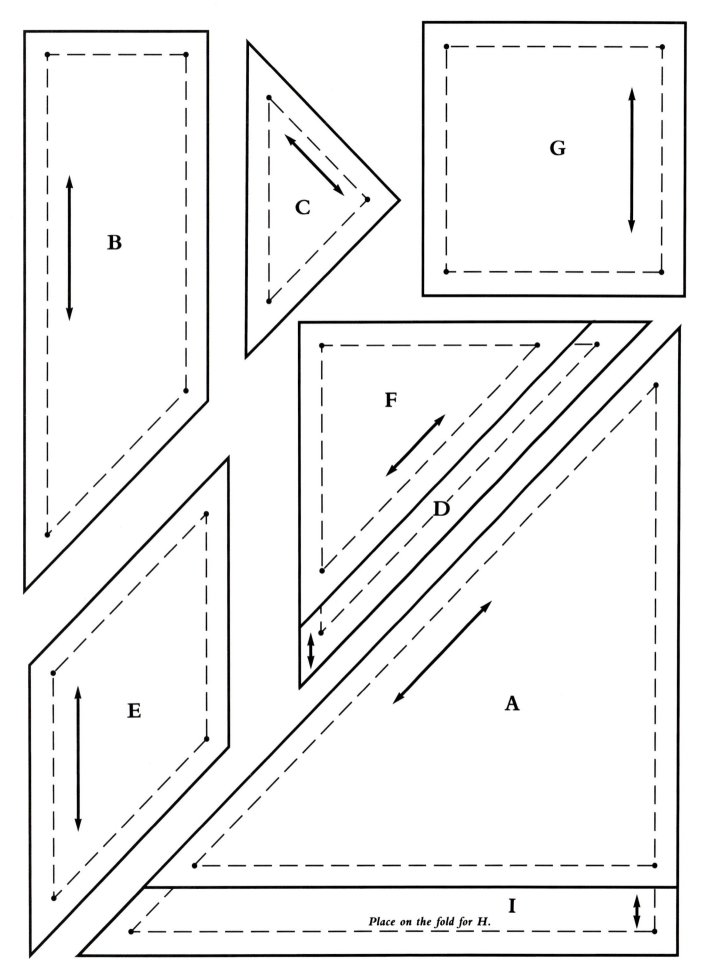

Place on the fold for H.

25

Sara Ann McLennand

Wellington, Florida

Can you remember the first quilt that really whetted your appetite for quilting? For Sara Ann it was an old tied quilt that covered her parents' bed. "I remember wondering about the origin of those two-inch fabric squares and trying to 'accidentally' make the tiny hole in the corner just a little bit bigger so that I could see and feel what was inside," she says.

Quilting became a big part of Sara Ann's life over 16 years ago. "I was absolutely fascinated by quilts and the methods of making them," she remembers. "I made many mistakes along the way. My first quilt had four batts in it! Quilts were supposed to be heavy, weren't they?"

Through a process of trial and error, Sara Ann has become an accomplished quilter, and she emphasizes the necessity for the documentation of all quilts. She reminds us, "If not preserved properly or documented in some way, your pieces of time, transposed into cloth and thread, are as fragile as the dreams they were based on."

Duck Island Basket
1988

If you are looking for a traditional basket with a handle, you won't find it in Sara Ann's *Duck Island Basket*. But once you realize that it is a coiled Indian basket design transformed into a quilted format, you'll say, "Oh, I see the basket now!" *Duck Island Basket* was a ribbon winner at the 4th Annual Show and Contest of the American Quilter's Society in 1988, but it holds an even more precious place in Sara Ann's heart than just being a ribbon winner. It represents her first break from traditional patterns. The quilt is named in memory of her grandparents and their cabin

(where she found the basket) on Duck Island in Michigan.

Duck Island Basket is made entirely of chintz. When using chintz, attention should be given to grain line direction. No grain line arrows are printed on the patterns since the direction of the grain changes with the piece's placement in the quilt. With chintz, all grain lines should go in the same direction, no matter where pieces are positioned; otherwise, the sheen of the fabric will reflect in different directions and detract from the quilt's overall appearance. Cutting pieces as you go, drafting the entire quilt before cutting, or arranging curved patterns in a circle as you cut them will be helpful. In addition, two borders of

a four-border set are cut across the grain and the opposing borders, with the grain.

Sara Ann recommends piecing the many small, intricate pieces by hand. "Accuracy is most important when piecing this design," she says.

Read more about Sara Ann's techniques for successfully making a quilt with curved piecing in our "Designer Gallery." There you can see the second quilt in her basket series, *Coiled Symmetry*.

Though we do not classify our quilts according to difficulty, we do not recommend this as your first quilt. To make the quilt easier to piece, our instructions and patterns omit the break in the basket "bottom" (rust circle).

Duck Island Basket

Finished Quilt Size
80″ x 80″

Additional Tools Required
Yardstick compass

Fabric Requirements*
Rust	—2¾ yd.
Dk. green	—4¾ yd.
Dk. red	—3 yd.
Black	—5¼ yd.**
Gold	—5½ yd.
Dk. red for bias binding	—1¼ yd.
Black for backing	—4¾ yd.

*All fabrics are chintz.
**See steps 3 and 7 before cutting fabric.

Number to Cut***
Template A	—1 gold
Template B	—10 gold
Template C	—10 gold
Template D	—10 gold
Template E	—10 gold
Template F	—10 black
Template G	—10 black
Template H	—10 black
Template I	—10 black
Template J	—13 black
Template K	—13 black
Template L	—13 black
Template M	—13 black
Template N	—13 gold
Template O	—13 gold
Template P	—13 gold
Template Q	—13 gold
Template R	—4 dk. green
Template S	—20 gold
	4 black
Template T	—20 gold
Template U	—12 gold
Template V	—4 gold
	—8 black
Template W	—8 black
Template X	—8 black
Template Y	—4 gold
Template Y‡	—4 gold
Template Z	—8 black
Template AA	—4 black
Template AA‡	—4 black
Template BB	—4 black
Template BB‡	—4 black
Template CC	—4 gold
Template DD	—12 gold
Template EE	—24 gold
Template FF	—24 gold
Template GG	—48 gold
Template HH	—48 gold
Template II	—24 gold
	36 black

Template JJ	—24 gold
Template KK	—36 black
Template LL	—36 black
Template MM	—12 black
Template NN	—24 black
Template OO	—24 black
Template PP	—24 black
Template QQ	—24 black
Template RR	—8 gold
Template SS	—8 gold
Template TT	—4 gold
Template UU	—4 black
Template VV	—4 black
Template WW	—4 black
Template XX	—8 black
Template YY	—8 black

***Review the narrative on page 26 and for *Coiled Symmetry* on page 141 before proceeding.
‡Flip or turn over template if fabric is one-sided.

Quilt Top Assembly
1. Alternate pieces (B) and (F) and join to make first circular row, as shown in Circle Piecing Diagram. Join row to circle (A). Continue in this manner for the next 3 rows, using pieces indicated on diagram and joining each row as completed to the preceding row.
2. Cut a one-piece circle with a 26½″ diameter from rust. Cut out center, leaving an unbroken 2½″-wide band. Join rust band to pieced circle.

An alternate method: Cut a 26½″ square from rust. Center pieced circle on square and appliqué to square. With yardstick compass, mark a 26½″ circle on quilt and trim corners. Cut fabric from behind pieced circle, leaving ¼″ seam allowance.
3. Cut a one-piece circle with a 30½″ diameter from black. Cut out center of circle, leaving an unbroken 2½″-wide band. Join black band to pieced circle. (You may use the appliqué method here also.)
4. Alternate pieces J and N and join to make a circular row, as shown in Circle Piecing Diagram. Continue as before, ending with a one-piece gold circular row with a 1″ finished width.

Join pieces (R) to circle to make a 40″ square (finished size).
5. Cut 4 borders, 2″ wide, from dk. red. Join to sides of quilt. Leave corners unstitched and unmitered because they will be trimmed after the next section is attached. (See quilt photograph and step 6.)
6. Alternate pieces (V) and (Z) with piece S, as shown in Triangle Section Piecing Diagram. Join pieces to make the first row. Continue

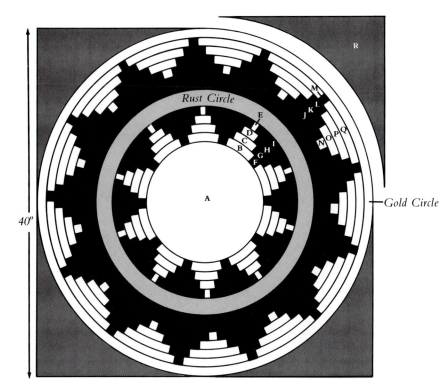

Circle Piecing Diagram

joining pieces to form rows, as shown, and join rows in the same manner as the pieced circle. Make 4 triangle sections.

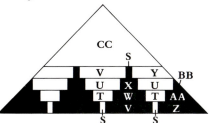

Triangle Section Piecing Diagram

Join sections to sides of quilt, as shown in Setting Diagram I. Trim dk. red borders, leaving ¼″ seam allowance.

Setting Diagram I

7. Cut 4 borders, 2½″ wide, from black. Join to quilt and miter corners.
8. Join pieces for border arches, as shown in Border Arch Piecing Diagram. Build arches in same manner as circle and triangles. Cut a 20½″

square from rust to make the last row. The rust arch is 2″ wide (finished size). Make 12 border arches.
9. Cut 2 rectangles, 15″ x 41″, and 2 rectangles, 22″ x 81″, all from dk. green for border background. (A special note to quilters: Sara Ann and the editor felt that the easiest way for you to assemble this border was to appliqué the arches to the background. This means that quite a bit of fabric is cut away after the borders are attached, leaving the quilter with excess fabric. We understand that many quilters may find this intolerable, but on the flip side, it will unify the border with a seamless background. There are alternative methods, but we chose the simplest.)

Finger-crease each rectangle in half widthwise. Place 3 arches side-by-side on each rectangle, centering the middle arch over finger-creased line, as shown in Border Assembly Diagrams. Leaving about a 2″ margin of fabric at the top of each rectangle, appliqué arches to fabric. Border Assembly Diagram II shows that only half of the end arches can be appliquéd to the background. These halves remain free until borders are joined to the quilt. (See Setting Diagrams II and III.)

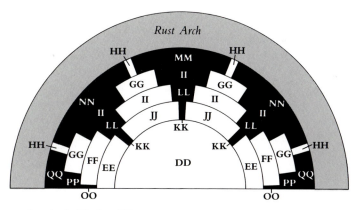

Border Arch Piecing Diagram

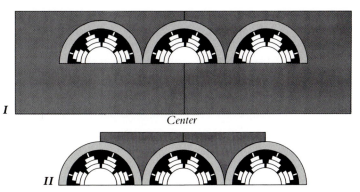

Border Assembly Diagrams

10. Join arches with longer rectangular backgrounds to quilt, as shown in Setting Diagram II.

Setting Diagram II

Join remaining arches to quilt, as shown in Setting Diagram III. Appliqué free edges of arches to background. It is the quilter's option to create a seam where the two background rectangles meet (marked with an X on diagram). The seam isn't required because when the final border is attached (step 12), this area becomes seam allowance. (See quilt photograph.) However, you may wish to baste this area for stabilization.

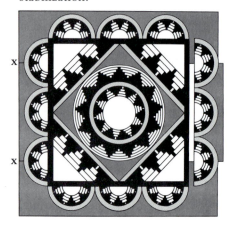

Setting Diagram III

Trim background fabric from behind arches and quilt only, leaving ¼" seam allowance. Background fabric for corners is trimmed after corner triangles are attached (step 11).

11. Join pieces for corner triangles in rows, as shown in Corner Triangle Piecing Diagram. Make 4 corner triangles.

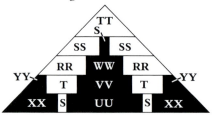

Corner Triangle Piecing Diagram

Join triangles to corners, as shown in Setting Diagram IV. Trim background fabric from behind triangles.

Setting Diagram IV

12. Cut 4 borders, 1½" wide, from dk. red. Join border so that its seam meets the top edge of each arch, and the border covers the place where background rectangles meet. Trim background fabric, leaving ¼" seam allowance. Miter corners.

Quilting
All quilting is done with black thread. Quilt in-the-ditch in the seam lines of circle, triangle sections, and border arches. Quilt lines parallel to this quilting, as shown in quilt photograph. Parallel lines of quilting are also done in background fabric of borders.

Finished Edges
Bind with dk. red fabric.

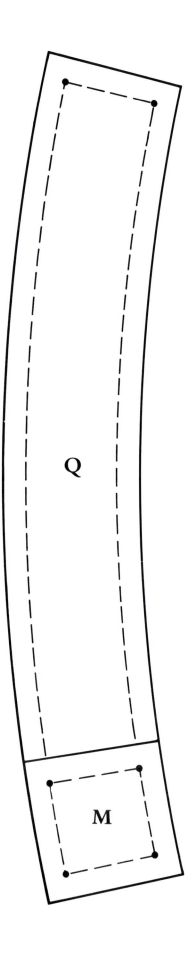

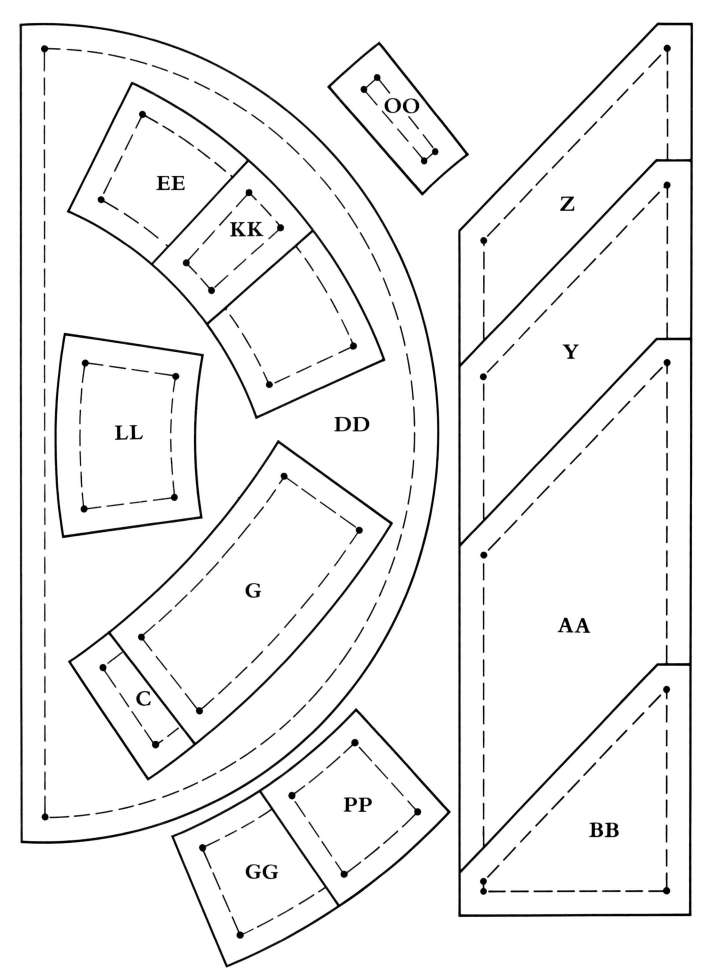

EE

OO

KK

Z

Y

LL

DD

G

AA

C

BB

GG

PP

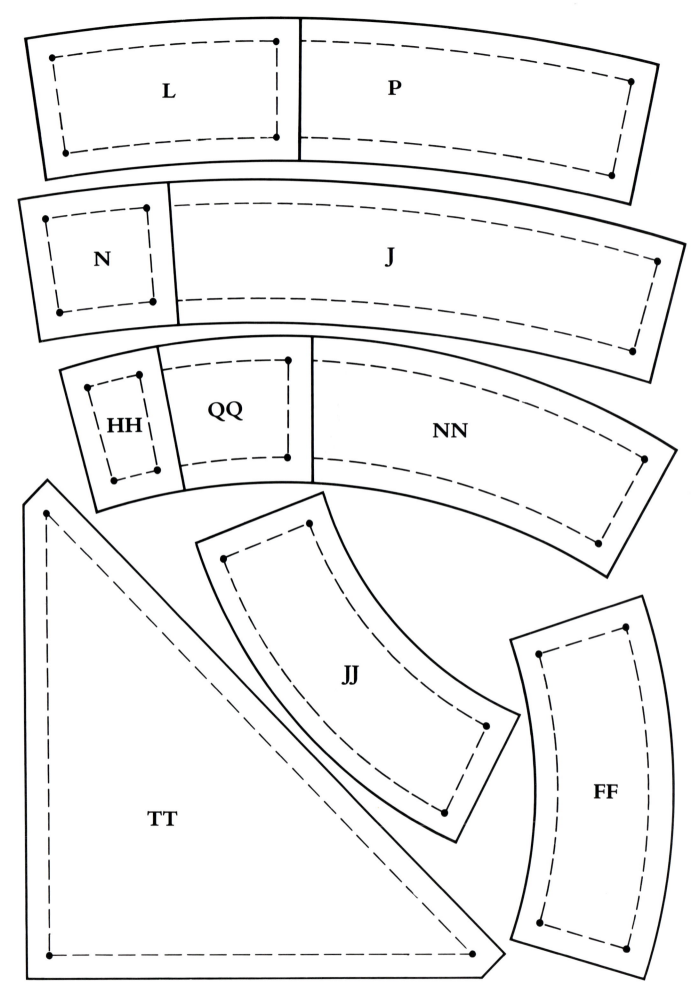

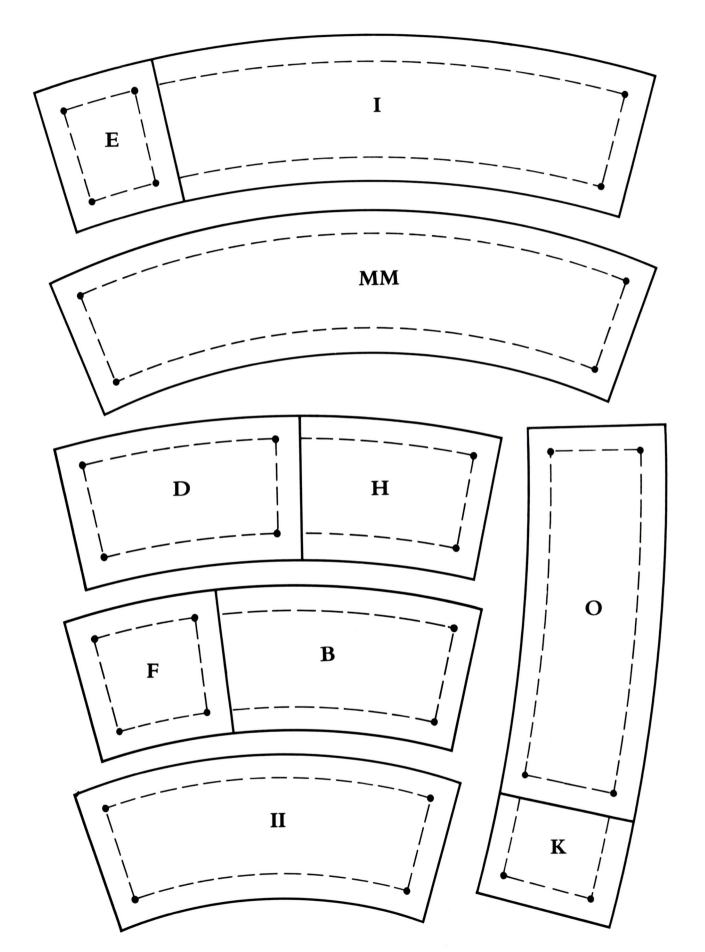

E

I

MM

D

H

O

F

B

II

K

33

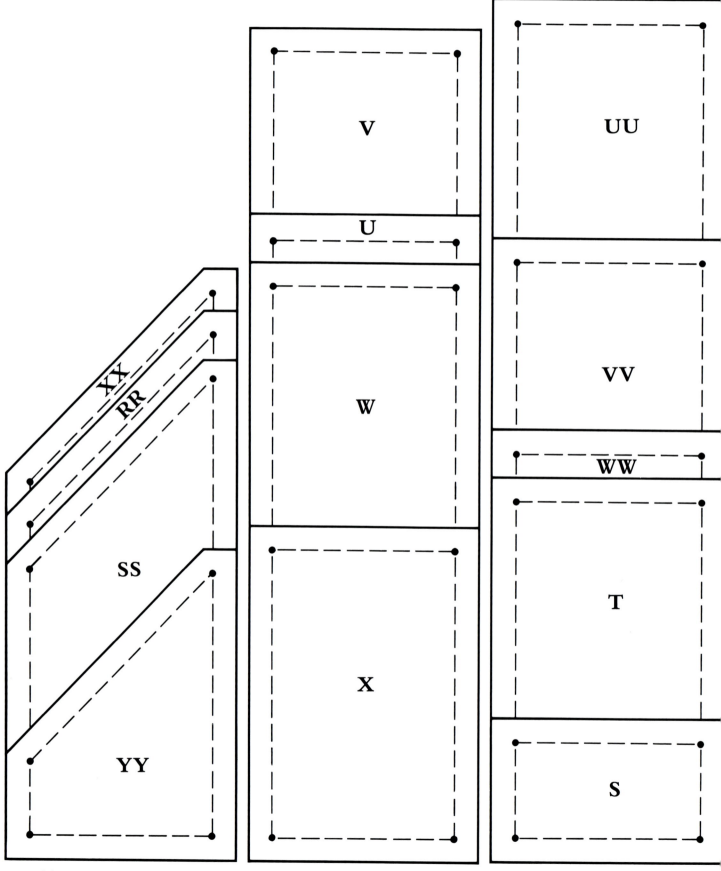

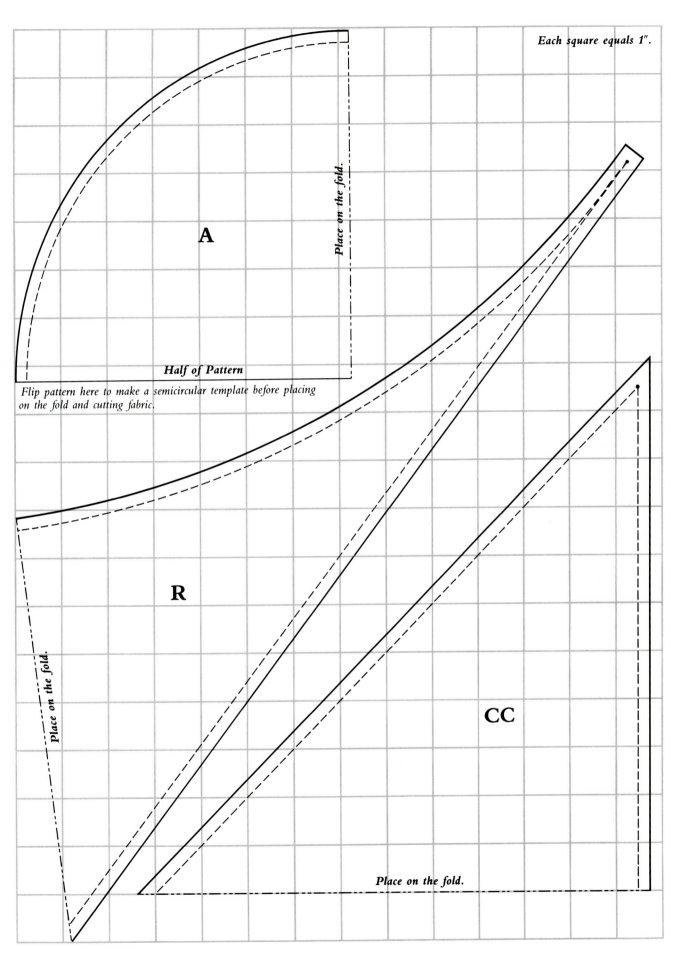

Each square equals 1".

A

Place on the fold.

Half of Pattern

Flip pattern here to make a semicircular template before placing on the fold and cutting fabric.

R

Place on the fold.

CC

Place on the fold.

35

Martha Waterman

Janesville, Iowa

When Martha is asked why she spends so much time cutting fabric into little pieces and putting them back together again, she promptly pulls out a ready-made comforter and compares it to a handmade quilt. Then she replies, "Now, which one would you rather have? I know which one I'd rather *make*—the quilt, every time!"

Martha says that one of the most interesting surprises of her life was discovering that she is a traditionalist. "As a young person," says Martha, "I loved new styles, city life, avant-garde ideas, wild colors and patterns, contemporary anything. It took me a while to realize that my heart was really in the timeless 'old ways' and the rural Iowa countryside."

During the day Martha works as the supervisor of the University of Northern Iowa's theater costume shop. But once away from the job, it's home to a simpler life in the country. "As I'm driving home," says Martha, "I almost always grin because the country-side's peacefulness gives everything I do a rhythm and an order." Quilting does much the same for her. "If I can come home to a quilt in the frame," she says, "life seems a little less hectic."

Corn and Cherries
1988

Sweet corn and cherry pie—not necessarily together—were two of Martha's favorite foods during her childhood. Growing up in Iowa, she acquired an appreciation for the land and the things the land pro-vided. Her Ribbon blocks represent Martha's native soil—the gentle roll of the hills, the twist of the creek, the wind of the road leading home, and the curve of the willow branch. "I am happy with this quilt," she says, "because it reflects the simple, rural life of my childhood and maintains the patchwork traditions of my family."

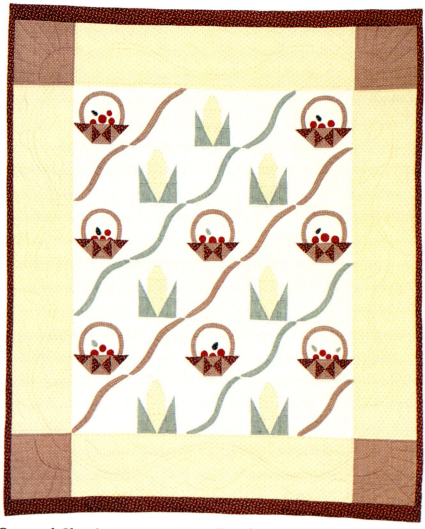

Quilt Top Assembly

1. Join pieces A through G into sections, as shown in Corn Block Piecing Diagrams I and II. Join sections to complete block. Make 7 Corn blocks.

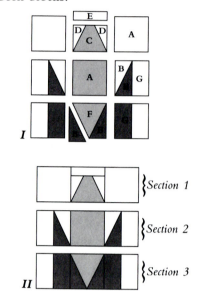

Corn Block Piecing Diagrams

2. Join triangles I and H to form basket base, as shown in Basket Block Piecing Diagrams.

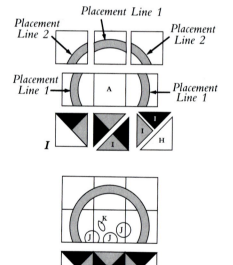

Basket Block Piecing Diagrams

Mark placement lines for handle on muslin squares (A), as shown in Basket Block Piecing Diagram I. Cut 8 bias strips, 1″ x 15″, from tan print for pieced-basket handles. Appliqué bias strip along placement lines of each square A. Join squares, matching handle seam lines as shown. (If you elect to appliqué a

Corn and Cherries

Finished Quilt Size
44″ x 50″

Number of Blocks and Finished Size
8 Basket blocks—6″ x 6″
7 Corn blocks—6″ x 6″
15 Ribbon blocks—6″ x 6″

Fabric Requirements
Yellow print	—1½ yd.
Tan print	—1⅛ yd.
Cranberry print	—1¾ yd.
Red pindot	—⅛ yd.
Dk. green print	—⅛ yd.
Green gingham (micro)	—¾ yd.
Muslin	—1½ yd.
Backing	—3 yd.★

★Or 1⅝ yd. of 60″-wide fabric

Number to Cut
Template A	—7 yellow print★★
	62 muslin★★★
Template B	—14 green gingham
	14 muslin
Template B‡	—14 green gingham
Template C	—7 yellow print★★
Template D	—14 muslin
Template E	—7 muslin
Template F	—7 yellow print★★
Template G	—14 green gingham
	28 muslin
Template H	—16 muslin
Template I	—32 tan print
	32 cranberry print★★
Template J	—24 red pindot
Template K	—3 green gingham
	5 dk. green print
Template L	—8 tan print
	7 green gingham
6½″ square	—15 muslin
7½″ square	—4 tan print

★★See step 5 and Finished Edges before cutting fabrics.
★★★Or cut 14 of template A and 8 rectangles, 4½″ x 6½″, from muslin. See step 2.
‡Flip or turn over template if fabric is one-sided.

38

one-piece handle, the handle can be cut from a 5½"-diameter circle [measurement includes seam allowances] and appliquéd to a 4½" x 6½" muslin rectangle. The finished width of the handle is ½".) Mark placement lines for cherries and leaf, using Placement Square. Martha wants quilters to know that these placement lines are only a suggestion. "The quilt is more lively with variations in cherry and leaf placement," says Martha. (Hint: A nickel is the same size as the finished cherry.) Appliqué cherries and leaf to block.

Join basket base to handle section, as shown in Basket Block Piecing Diagrams. Make 8 Basket blocks.

3. Appliqué ribbon (L) to 6½" muslin squares, as shown in quilt photograph.

4. Arrange blocks in 6 rows of 5 blocks each, as shown in quilt photograph. Join blocks at sides to form rows. Join rows.

5. Cut 2 borders, 7½" x 36½", from yellow print. Join to opposite sides of quilt.

Cut 2 borders, 7½" x 30½", from yellow print. Join 7½" tan print squares to opposite ends of yellow print borders. Join borders to top and bottom of quilt.

Quilting
Outline-quilt ¼" inside seam lines of all basket base pieces. Outline-quilt ¼" outside seam lines of handle. Outline-quilt inside seam lines of handle, cherries, and leaf.

Outline-quilt ¼" inside seam lines of corn leaves and cob. Outline-quilt ¼" outside seam line of corn shape. Outline-quilt inside seam line of ribbon.

Echo-quilt the curve of the ribbon (L) in the remainder of the Ribbon block area. (Echo-quilting lines are ⅝" apart.)

Mark a rising sun in each tan print corner square for quilting by drawing an arc for the sun in the corner of each square (a portion of a circle with a 4" radius is best). Draw straight lines for rays from arc to complete your rising sun.

Quilt a vine with leaves and tendrils for borders.

Finished Edges
Cut 2 strips for side bindings, 1½" wide, from cranberry print. Turn

lengthwise raw edges under ¼" and press. Use crease as guide for seam. With right sides facing, join bindings to opposite sides of quilt so that seam line is ¾" from edge of quilt. Turn bindings to back of quilt and blindstitch folded edge to quilt.

Cut 2 strips for top and bottom bindings, 2¾" wide, from cranberry print. Repeat as above, but join bindings to quilt so that seam line is 1¾" from edge of quilt.

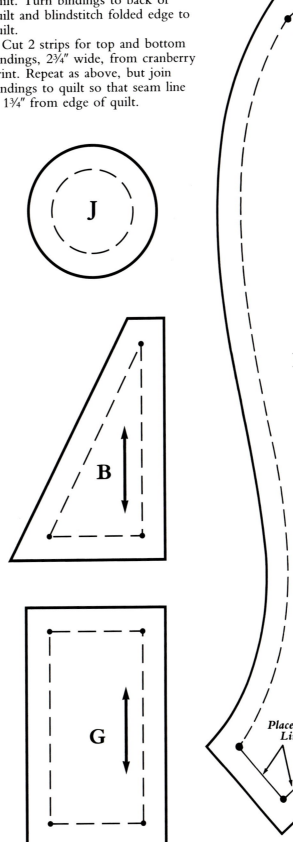

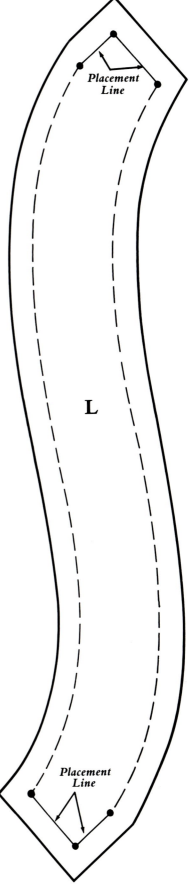

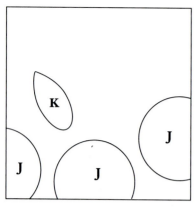

Placement Square

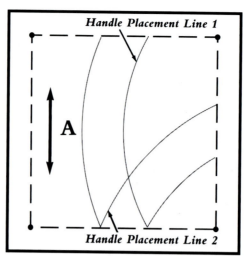

Handle Placement Line 1

A

Handle Placement Line 2

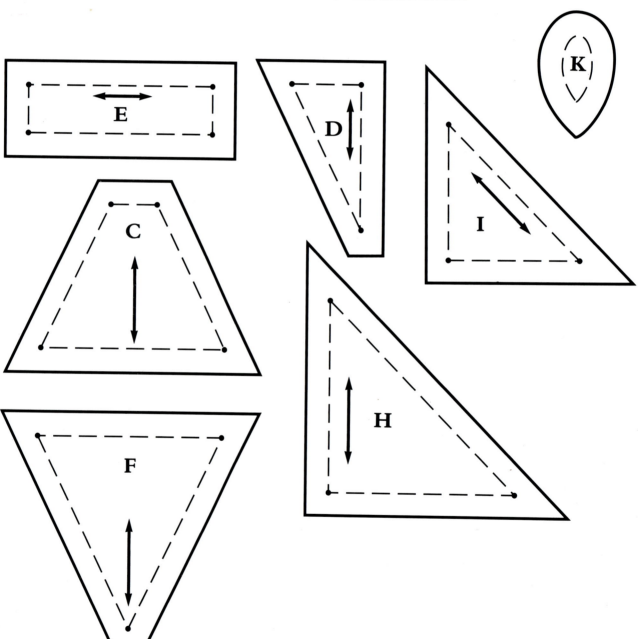

K

E

D

C

I

F

H

"The problems I encountered with my first quilt," says Merrilyn, "made me realize that there was more to quiltmaking than I had thought." A few quilts later, she struck up a friendship with the owner of a new quilt shop in town. She began making items for display at the shop; and gradually, her work and responsibilities increased. "The next thing I knew," says Merrilyn, "I had resigned from my job as an elementary school teacher and was working in the shop!"

The shop has since closed, but the job provided an avenue for Merrilyn to begin teaching others to quilt and an inspiration for her to pursue her own talents. "I never tire of this pleasant medium," says Merrilyn, "because it allows me to create something that captures a small part of my life."

Merrilyn O. San Soucie
Newmarket, New Hampshire

Cyclical Basketry
1984

The cyclical changing of the seasons is expressed in fabric and color in Merrilyn's *Cyclical Basketry*. "The basket pattern has always been one of my favorites," she says, "and I found it quite challenging to use baskets to express the seasons in fabric."

Merrilyn reminds us that it is important to choose fabrics for this quilt that are nearly equal in print size and color depth. (She used traditional calicoes.) Review the Number to Cut for Baskets section and the quilt photograph before selecting fabrics. Each block contains a dark, a medium, and a light print. The borders are Merrilyn's original patchwork design and were planned to incorporate the four main color groups in the quilt and enhance the central design.

Cyclical Basketry

Finished Quilt Size
34⅝″ x 34⅝″

**Number of Blocks and
Finished Size**
4 blocks—8″ x 8″

Fabric Requirements

Muslin	—⅝ yd.
Green print I	—⅜ yd.
Green print II	—⅛ yd.
Dk. green print	—⅛ yd.
Yellow print	—⅜ yd.
Peach print	—⅛ yd.
Brown print	—¼ yd.
Tan print	—⅜ yd.
Beige/brown print I	—¼ yd.
Beige/brown print II	—⅛ yd.
Beige/gray print	—⅛ yd.
Gray print I	—⅜ yd.
Gray print II	—⅛ yd.
Dk. rust print	—⅛ yd.
Umber	—⅛ yd.
Muslin for binding	—1 yd.
Backing	—1¼ yd.

Number to Cut for Baskets
Yellow Basket

Template A	—1 yellow print
Template B	—1 muslin
Template C	—1 yellow print
Template D	—1 yellow print
	1 beige/brown print I
Template D★	—1 yellow print
	1 beige/brown print I
Template E	—1 yellow print
Template G	—2 peach print
Template H	—2 muslin
Template I	—1 yellow print
	1 muslin
Template J	—4 yellow print

Green Basket

Template A	—1 dk. green print
Template B	—1 muslin
Template C	—1 green print I
Template D	—1 green print I
	1 green print II
Template D★	—1 green print I
	1 green print II
Template E	—1 green print I
Template G	—2 dk. green print
Template H	—2 muslin
Template I	—1 green print I
	1 muslin
Template J	—4 green print I

Brown Basket

Template A	—1 brown print
Template B	—1 muslin
Template C	—1 tan print
Template D	—1 tan print
	1 beige/brown print II
Template D★	—1 tan print
	1 beige/brown print II
Template E	—1 tan print
Template G	—2 brown print
Template H	—2 muslin
Template I	—1 tan print
	1 muslin
Template J	—4 tan print

Gray Basket

Template A	—1 beige/gray print
Template B	—1 muslin
Template C	—1 gray print I
Template D	—1 gray print I
	1 beige/gray print
Template D★	—1 gray print I
	1 beige/gray print
Template E	—1 gray print I
Template G	—2 gray print II
Template H	—2 muslin
Template I	—1 gray print I
	1 muslin
Template J	—4 gray print I

Number to Cut for Remainder of Quilt

Template C	—8 green print I
	8 dk. rust print
Template D	—4 dk. rust print
Template D★	—4 dk. rust print
Template E	—4 muslin
	8 beige/brown print I
	8 gray print I
Template F	—4 muslin
Template I	—4 brown print
Template K	—8 tan print
	8 yellow print
	16 gray print I
	16 muslin
Template L	—16 beige/brown print I
Template M	—16 green print I
	8 tan print
	8 yellow print
Template N	—16 muslin
Template O	—8 brown print
Template P	—8 yellow print
	4 green print I
Template Q	—4 peach print
Template Q★	—4 peach print
Template R	—4 umber
Template S	—8 muslin
Template T	—4 muslin
8½″ square	—1 muslin

★Flip or turn over template if fabric is one-sided.

Quilt Top Assembly

1. Sort pieces into groups for basket blocks as listed above. Join pieces, as shown in Block Piecing Diagram. Frame each block with pieces J.

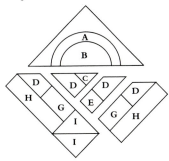

Block Piecing Diagram

2. Join square and triangles (F, T) to basket blocks, as shown in Setting Diagram I.

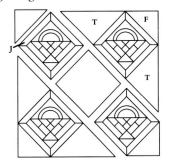

Setting Diagram I

3. Join pieces (K, L, M, and N) to make pieced border rectangles, as shown in Border Piecing Diagram.

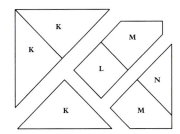

Border Piecing Diagram

Make 4 using gray print I triangles (K) with tan print pieces (M); make 4 using tan print triangles (K) with green print I pieces (M); make 4 using yellow print triangles (K) with green print I pieces (M); make 4 using gray print I triangles (K) with yellow print pieces (M).

4. Join pieces, as shown in Flower Block Piecing Diagram. Make 4.

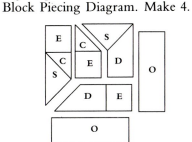

Flower Block Piecing Diagram

5. Arrange border rectangles and flower blocks, as shown in quilt photograph and Setting Diagram II.

Setting Diagram II

Join 4 border rectangles, as shown, for each border. Join 2 borders to opposite sides of quilt. Join flower blocks to the ends of the remaining borders. Join borders to top and bottom of quilt, as shown.

6. Join pieces as shown in Corner Block Piecing Diagram. Make 4.

Corner Block Piecing Diagram

Join pieces (P, Q, and R) for border strips, as shown in Setting Diagram III. Join border strips to quilt sides first.

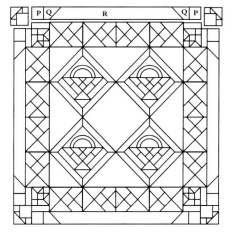

Setting Diagram III

Set-in corner blocks by stitching from the outside edge up to the seam line. Stop and backstitch 1 or 2 stitches. Remove fabric from the machine. Align the remaining sides and stitch from the center to the outside edge, backstitching 1 or 2 stitches at the start.

Quilting

Outline-quilt outside seam lines of all basket pieces. Outline-quilt ¼″ inside seam lines of all border pieces. Duplicate basket design in quilting in the muslin center square. Quilt half-baskets in triangles (T). Duplicate flower motif from flower block in quilting in each triangle (F).

Finished Edges

Bind with muslin.

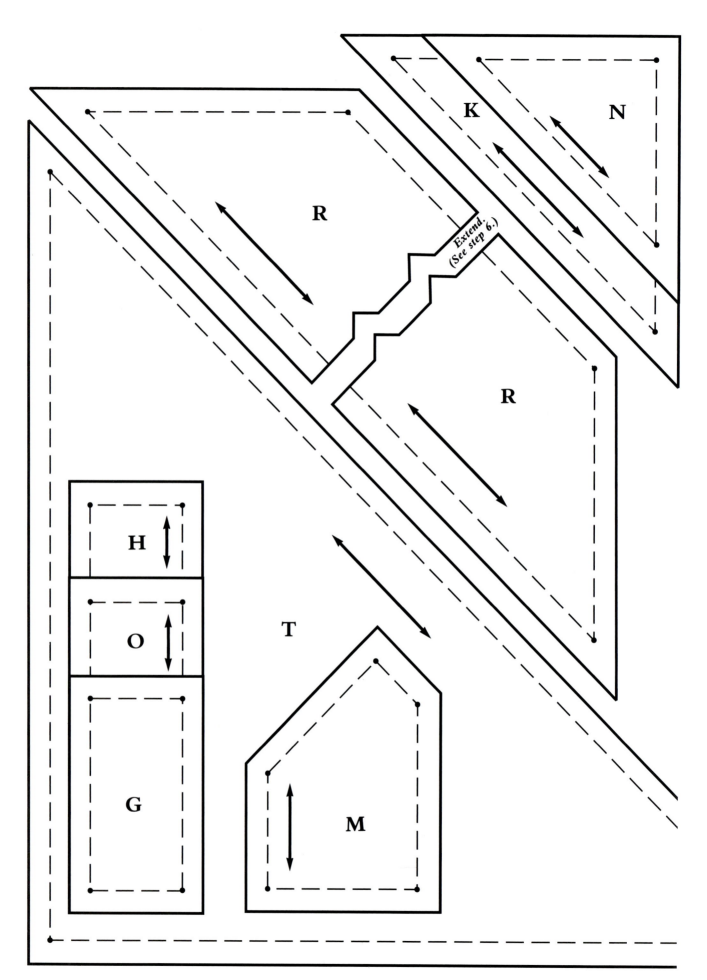

K

N

R

Extend.
(See step 6.)

R

H

O

T

G

M

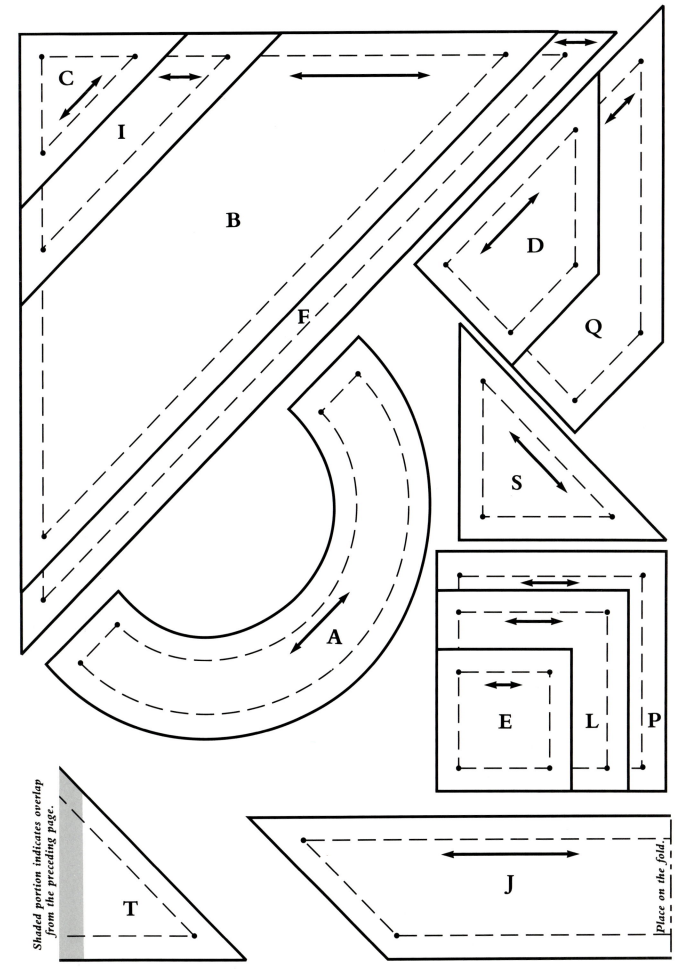

C

I

B

F

D

Q

A

S

E L P

Shaded portion indicates overlap from the preceding page.

T

J

Place on the fold.

45

QUILTS
ACROSS
AMERICA

4. Join 6 segments at sides 4 times each to make 4 borders, as shown in Setting Diagram. Join borders to top and bottom of quilt, as shown.

Make 4 corner blocks, as shown in Corner Block Piecing Diagram.

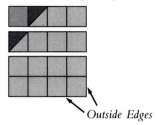

Outside Edges

Corner Block Piecing Diagram

(Use a single green print for triangles in each corner block.) Join corner blocks to opposite ends of remaining borders, as shown in Setting Diagram. Join borders to quilt.

Corner Block *Border Segment*

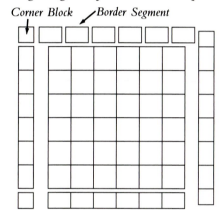

Setting Diagram

Quilting
Outline-quilt ¼″ outside seam lines, as shown in Quilting Diagram. Quilt feather and heart patterns, as shown.

Finished Edges
Bind with blue print fabric.

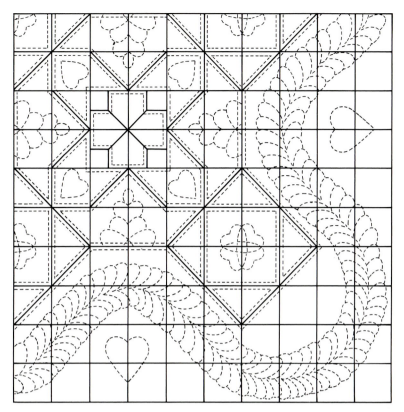

Quilting Diagram

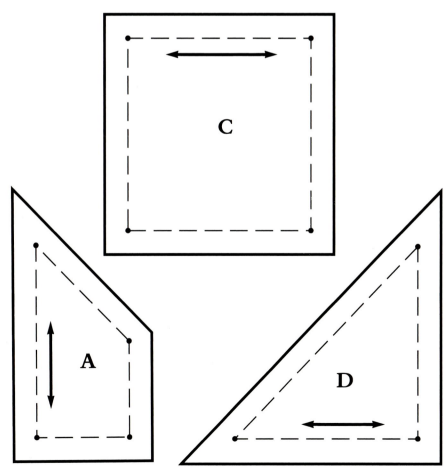

Lois Richichi

Roslyn, Pennsylvania

Template-free! That's the way to go for Lois. Stimulated by the patterns of antique quilts, Lois challenges herself to figure out a method for duplicating them without using templates. "When you have a million quilting ideas rolling around in your head," she says, "template-free, machine-pieced quiltmaking is the only way to see them all through in a lifetime."

Lois admits, "Quilting didn't come easy to me. I was the most inept student in my class!" But because of this, she has become an excellent quilting teacher, who focuses on encouraging her students to persevere. She often tells her students, "If I can do this, anyone can."

Vintage Plaids
1990

Here's your chance to shake the cobwebs off your scrap basket and pull out those plaids! *Vintage Plaids* is Lois's adaptation of an antique quilt that used hundreds of plaids. She reorganized the setting and developed a template-free method for making it. She wanted to show her quilting class that the look of an antique quilt could be reproduced in a fraction of the time it would take using templates. She assures us that the top for *Vintage Plaids* can be made in 8 hours. "In addition," says Lois, "a smaller wall hanging can be made by stopping at the sashing."

Vintage Plaids

Finished Quilt Size
45″ x 50″

Number of Blocks and Finished Size
40 blocks—5″ x 5″

Fabric Requirements

Plaids★	—1½ yd. total
Muslin★★	—1¼ yd.
Red	—1⅜ yd.
Plaid for bias binding	—¾ yd.
Ticking stripe for backing	—3 yd.★★★

★At least ⅓ yard each of 4 different plaids is required.
★★Use tea-dyed or unbleached muslin.
★★★If fabric is wider than 45″, 1¾ yards will be sufficient.

Quilt Top Assembly

1. Cut 1 strip across the grain, 5⅞″ wide, from each plaid. Cut strips into twenty 5⅞″ squares. Cut squares on the diagonal to make 40 triangles and set aside.

2. Cut a total of 5 strips across the grain, 3⅜″ wide, from plaids. Cut 5 strips across the grain, 3⅜″ wide, from muslin.

To make pieced squares, place 1 plaid strip and 1 muslin strip together with right sides facing. Draw vertical lines on muslin strip in 3⅜″ increments, as shown in Pieced Triangles Diagram. Draw diagonal lines, as shown. Draw broken lines ¼″ on each side of solid diagonal lines, as shown. Stitch on broken lines. Cut strips on all solid diagonal and straight lines. Repeat for other strips. Make 108 pieced squares and set aside.

Pieced Triangles Diagram

3. Cut 4 strips, 3⅜″ wide, from muslin. Cut forty 3⅜″ squares. Cut squares on the diagonal to make 80 triangles.

4. Join muslin triangles to sides of 40 pieced squares, as shown in Block Piecing Diagram. Join large triangles, cut in step 1, to complete blocks, as shown.

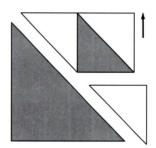

Block Piecing Diagram

5. Arrange blocks for color placement in 5 vertical rows before joining. Join blocks at sides, as shown in Setting Diagram I.

6. Cut 6 strips for sashing, 3″ wide, from red. Alternate sashing with block rows, as shown in Setting Diagram I. (Note that the direction of block rows is alternated.) Join rows to sashing.

7. Cut 2 strips for top and bottom sashing, 3″ wide, from red. Join to quilt, as shown in Setting Diagram I.

8. Join 18 pieced squares for side border, as shown in Setting Diagram II. Make 2 and join to opposite sides of quilt, as shown in Setting Diagram II.

9. Join 16 pieced squares for top border, as shown in Setting Diagram II. Repeat for bottom border. Cut four 3″ squares from muslin. Join squares to opposite ends of borders, as shown. Join borders to quilt.

Quilting

Outline-quilt ¼″ inside seam lines of all triangles. An unbroken cable is quilted on all sashing.

Finished Edges

Bind with plaid fabric.

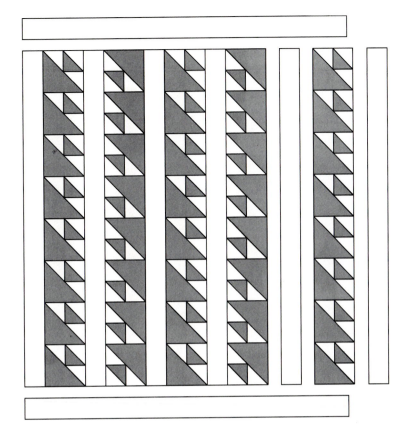

Setting Diagram I

Setting Diagram II

Margie Turner Karavitis
Spokane, Washington

Margie credits her quilt group with playing a large role in increasing her knowledge of quiltmaking. "I learned to quilt by trial and error (mostly error)," she says, "but it was not until I joined a quilt group that I had access to classes, books, and other quilters."

Several years ago Margie retired from a nursing career, and since then, her sometime hobby of quilting has turned into a life-style. "I plan vacations around quilt conferences," she says, "and I find that I would rather go to a quilt show than a play, a concert, or a movie."

She is a member of the Washington State Quilters, Spokane Chapter, and her ribbon-winning quilts are an inspiration to all.

Cherry Rose
1990

Margie is not shy when it comes to hand quilting. Following tradition, she has covered *Cherry Rose* with loads of it. Her small stitches and her careful selection of areas for corded quilting indicate a respect for the art of fine quiltmaking.

Cherry Rose won First Place and Best in the Arts and Crafts division at the Spokane Interstate Fair in 1990 and several Viewers' Choice ribbons at local quilt shows.

This is Margie's first attempt at making an appliquéd quilt. Margie, if this was your first, we can't wait to see what's next!

Cherry Rose

Finished Quilt Size
94⅜" x 94⅜"

Number of Blocks and Finished Size
16 blocks—18" x 18"

Fabric Requirements
Red — 2¼ yd.
Green print — 3⅛ yd. ★
Muslin — 7 yd.
Muslin for
  bias binding — 1¼ yd.
Backing — 8⅛ yd.
★Set aside 1 yard for making
¾"-wide bias for border vine.

Other Materials
Freezer paper
Fabric-compatible glue stick
  (optional)
Posterboard (optional)
Tapestry needle
White polyester cable cord, size 16
  (1/16" diameter)

Number to Cut
Template A — 80 red★★
Template B — 64 green print★★
Template C — 64 green print★★
Template D — 952 red★★
Template E — 464 green print★★
Template F — 200 muslin
              200 red
Template G — 40 green print★★
★★See steps 2 and 5 before cutting fabrics.

Quilt Top Assembly
1. Cut sixteen 18½" squares from muslin. Finger-crease squares on the diagonal; then finger-crease on the opposite diagonal to form guidelines for appliqué. Finger-crease squares in half twice for additional guidelines.
2. Trace pattern pieces A through E without seam allowance on dull side of freezer paper. (Margie suggests using a posterboard template for circles instead of freezer paper. See page 12, *Wicker Baskets*, step 1 for instructions.) Make number of each piece listed above and mark grain line arrows on each piece. Cut out pieces on traced lines. Press pieces, shiny side down, on wrong side of fabric. Cut fabric, adding ¼" seam allowance. Turn seam allowance to back of paper and baste or glue seam allowance in place.
  Arrange pieces on muslin square,

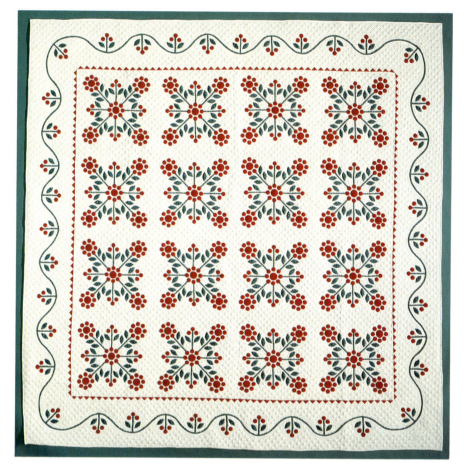

as shown in Placement Diagram. Layer-appliqué pieces in place. (Numbers in parentheses in Placement Diagram indicate the order for appliquéing.) The distance from midpoint of corner circle (A) to corner of square is 4½". The distance from midpoint of outer cherry (D) to side of square is 2½". Cut out fabric from behind pieces, leaving a ¼" seam allowance, and remove freezer paper or posterboard. Repeat for all 16 muslin squares.
3. Arrange blocks into 4 rows of 4 blocks each. Join blocks at sides to

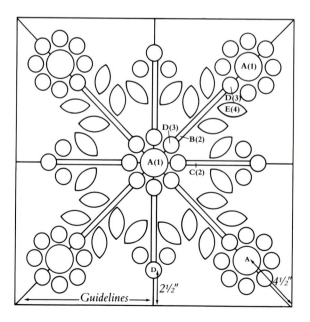

Placement Diagram

58

form a row; then join rows.

4. Alternate 50 red triangles (F) with 48 muslin triangles (F). Join triangles at sides to form a strip, beginning with a red triangle, as shown in Triangle Strip Diagram. Make 4 strips. Join strips to sides of quilt with muslin triangles on outside edges.

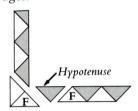

Triangle Strip Diagram

Join 2 muslin triangles (F) at sides, as shown in Triangle Strip Diagram. Make 4. Join to corners of quilt, as shown.

5. Cut 4 borders, 11″ wide, from muslin. Join to quilt and miter corners. Measuring from triangle strip border to triangle strip border, divide each border into 10 segments, as shown in Border Placement Diagram, and mark fabric lightly. (These lines will be the placement lines for cherry clusters.)

Prepare pieces D, G, and E, as above, and arrange them on border. For cherry clusters close to inside of quilt, the distance from midpoint of cherry (D) to outer seam of triangle strip border is 3″. For clusters close to outside edge of quilt, the distance from midpoint of cherry (D) to outside edge is 3½″. Layer-appliqué stems (G), cherries (D), and leaves (E) to border in that order. Center a cluster in each corner on the mitering seam. Cut out fabric from behind pieces, leaving a ¼″ seam allowance, and remove freezer paper or posterboard.

Make ¾″-wide bias strip from green print for vine. (Measurement includes seam allowances.) Weave vine around clusters, as shown in quilt photograph, and appliqué in place.

Quilting
Outline-quilt outside seam line of all appliquéd pieces. Outline-quilt inside seam line of all muslin triangles. For corded quilting, trace leaf pattern (E) between stems on each block. Quilt leaf along traced lines and outline-quilt ⅛″ inside first quilting line. Thread tapestry needle

with cord and insert needle from back of quilt ¼″ from start of design. (This prevents a large hole from forming when the needle is entered and exited in the same place.) Run cord through channel created by the lines of quilting until leaf shape is complete. Exit through back of quilt. Trim cord and tuck inside quilt. (Many quilters recommend leaving a generous trimmed edge of cording, since the cord may

shrink if the quilt is washed.) With your needle, gently straighten fabric fibers to camouflage the entrance and exit sites.

Echo-quilt 2 lines outside vine and border cherry clusters at ¼″ intervals. Quilt the remainder of the quilt with a 1″ double cross-hatching grid.

Finished Edges
Bind with muslin.

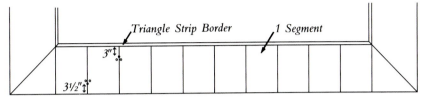

Border Placement Diagram

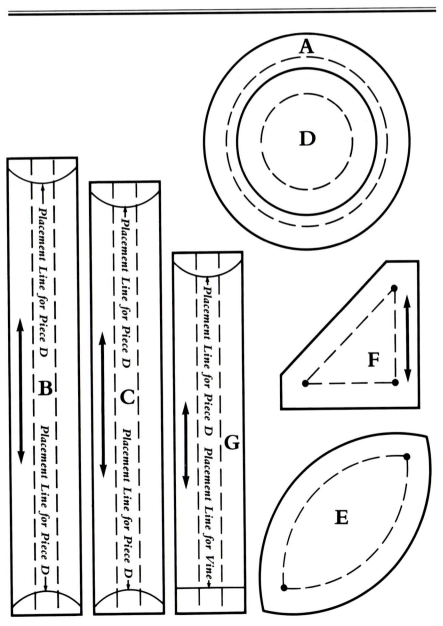

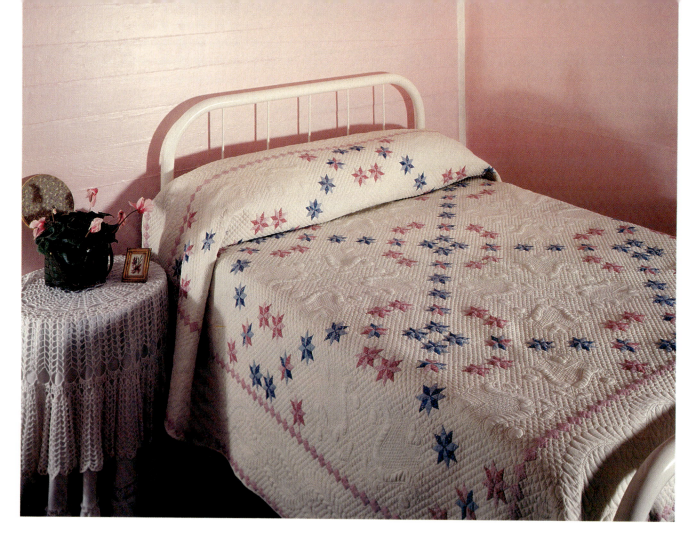

Oh, My Stars!
1989

Just let the ribbons do the talking. Margie says that she finds it easier to make a quilt than to talk about it. But, when you make a quilt like *Oh, My Stars!*, there's no need to talk. *Oh, My Stars!* won First Place in the Traditional Pieced, Professional category at the 6th Annual American Quilter's Society Show, Paducah, Kentucky, in 1990; Judges Recognition award by the National Quilting Association in 1990; First Place in Large Quilt Division at the Festival of the American West, 1990; and First Place and Best of Class at the Spokane Interstate Fair, 1990.

Margie was inspired to make *Oh, My Stars!* after seeing an antique scrap quilt of similar design. She selected pink and blue fabrics instead of using scraps and rearranged the setting to provide more space for quilting.

When a friend's husband first saw Margie's quilt, he exclaimed, "Oh, my stars!" Thus, the quilt's name was born.

Oh, My Stars!

Finished Quilt Size
94½" x 94½"

Number of Blocks and Finished Size
32 blocks—9" x 9"

Fabric Requirements
Muslin	—8½ yd.
Blue print	—¾ yd.
Lt. blue print	—¾ yd.
Dk. pink print	—¾ yd.
Pink print	—1½ yd.
Muslin for bias binding	—1¼ yd.
Backing	—8⅛ yd.

Other Materials
Tapestry needle
White polyester cable cord, size 16 (¹/₁₆" diameter)

Number to Cut
Template A	—320 blue print
	320 lt. blue print
	320 dk. pink print
	320 pink print
Template B	—640 muslin★
Template C	—640 muslin★
Template D	—128 muslin★
Template E	—480 pink print
Template F	—960 muslin★

★See steps 4 and 6 before cutting fabric.

Quilt Top Assembly
1. Alternate 2 pink print diamonds (A) with 2 dk. pink print diamonds (A) to form a half star, as shown in Star Square Piecing Diagram. Make 2. Join half stars. Join squares (B) and triangles (C) to complete square. Make 64 pink print star squares, 64 blue print star squares, and 32 pink print/blue print star squares. Refer to quilt photograph and Block Piecing Diagram for proper color placement.

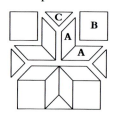

Star Square Piecing Diagram

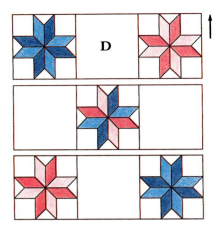

Block Piecing Diagram

2. Alternate star squares with squares (D), as shown in Block Piecing Diagram. Join squares in 3 rows and join rows. Make 32 blocks. (Arrow indicates top of block.)

3. Make 5 four-block sections, positioning blocks as shown in Four-Block Setting Diagram.

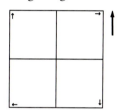

Four-Block Setting Diagram

4. Cut 8 rectangles, 9½" x 18½", from muslin. Cut four 18½" squares from muslin.

Alternate 4 blocks with 2 muslin rectangles for rows 1 and 5, as shown in Setting Diagram. Position each block as indicated by the arrow and join.

Arrange 2 four-block sections, 2 muslin rectangles, and 1 muslin square each for rows 2 and 4, as shown in Setting Diagram, and join.

Arrange 1 four-block section, 4 blocks, and 2 muslin squares for row 3, as shown in Setting Diagram, and join. Join rows.

5. For pieced-border strip, alternate 53 pink print squares (E) with 106 muslin triangles (F). Begin with a triangle joined to a square, as shown in Border Strip Piecing Diagram. Make 4 and join to sides of quilt.

Border Strip Piecing Diagram

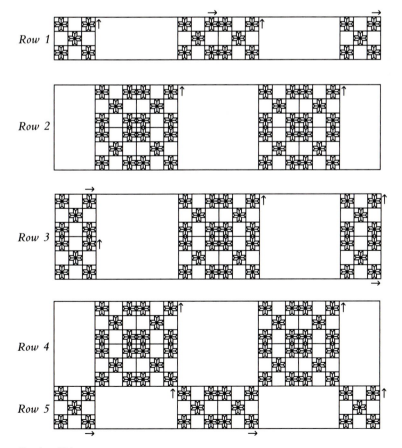

Row 1

Row 2

Row 3

Row 4

Row 5

Setting Diagram

6. Cut 4 borders, 9″ wide, from muslin. Join to quilt and miter corners.

7. Alternate 67 pink print squares (E) with 134 muslin triangles (F) and join as above. Make 4 and join to sides of quilt.

Quilting

Outline-quilt outside seam lines of all stars and squares (E).

Margie chose a stylized-tulip quilting pattern for her muslin squares and rectangles. The outline of the pattern is emphasized with corded quilting. (See quilting instructions for Margie's *Cherry Rose* for technique.) Trapunto and stipple quilting are used in the rest of the pattern. (See photograph of Margie's quilting.)

Intertwining feather quilting is used on the borders. The remainder of the quilt is quilted with a ½″ cross-hatching grid. Margie left all stars and squares (E) unquilted to give them a padded appearance.

Finished Edges

Bind with muslin.

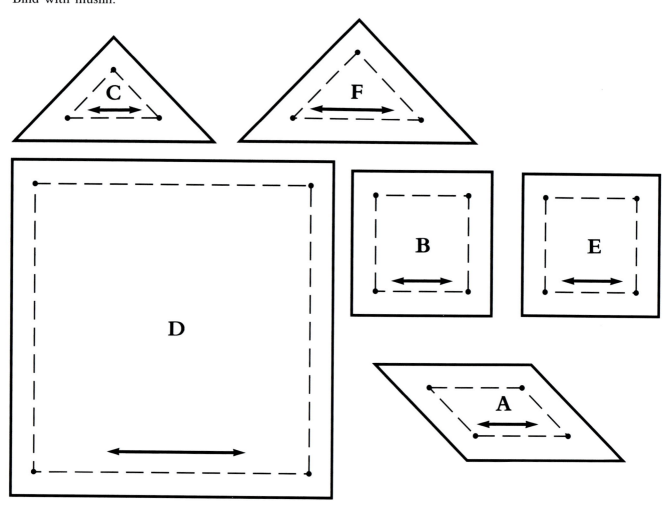

"They don't give out blue ribbons for clean windows and laundry," says Sandra. Quilting has become to her what it has to many—an outlet for self-expression and a satisfying pastime. "It has given me an identity besides that of being someone's mom or wife," she says.

Every facet of quiltmaking appeals to Sandra. "When I am designing the quilt, I can't wait to start cutting the fabric," she says. "After I start cutting the pieces, I get anxious to start sewing. While I'm sewing, I'm looking forward to quilting. Finally, when I begin to think I just can't quilt another stitch, the quilt is finished, and I generally have the next design floating around in my head."

Sandra Gould
Sussex, New Jersey

Whirligig in a Summer Breeze
1988

This entrancing wall hanging is an example of Sandra's ability as a designer and as a piecer. She modified the Pinwheel block, originally published by Delores Hinson in 1966, and spun two blocks from one. (See "Resources.") Precise piecing is necessary for this whirling pattern, and Sandra's selective placement of quilting lines illustrates how quilting can reinforce the patchwork design.

Whirligig in a Summer Breeze won blue ribbons at both the Warwick Valley Quilter's Guild Show in 1988, and the Sussex County Farm and Horse Show in 1989.

Whirligig in a Summer Breeze

Finished Quilt Size
53¼″ x 43¼″

Number of Blocks and Finished Size
63 blocks—5″ x 5″

Fabric Requirements

Yellow	— ¾ yd.
Pink plaid	— ¼ yd.
Pink/blue floral print	— ¼ yd.
Med. blue floral print	— 1¾ yd.
Blue	— 1⅝ yd.
Cream print	— 1⅝ yd.
Blue for bias binding	— 1 yd.
Backing	— 2⅝ yd.

Number to Cut

Template A	— 128 blue
Template B	— 64 cream print
	64 med. blue floral print
Template C	— 128 blue
Template D	— 64 med. blue floral print
	60 cream print
Template E	— 124 yellow
Template F	— 64 pink plaid
	60 pink/blue floral print

Quilt Top Assembly

1. Join pieces A through C, as shown in Block X Piecing Diagram. Pay particular attention to color arrangement and match marks on curves for accurate piecing. Sandra suggests clipping seam allowances on concave curves of pieces A and B, 1/16″ to 1/8″ deep, to ease fabric when joining. Make 32 of Block X. (Arrow indicates top of block.)

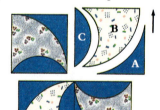

Block X Piecing Diagram
Make 32.

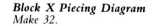
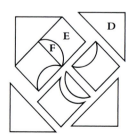

Block Y and Z Piecing Diagram

2. Join pieces D through F, as shown in Blocks Y and Z Piecing Diagram. Note the different color arrangements for Blocks Y and Z. Match marks on curves for accurate piecing and make the number of blocks indicated.

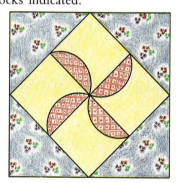

Block Y
Make 16.

Block Z
Make 15.

64

3. Arrange blocks X, Y, and Z in 7 rows of 9 blocks each, as shown in Setting Diagram. Note the placement of block X. Join blocks at sides to form rows and join rows.

X↑	Y	X↑	Y	X↑	Y	X↑	Y	X↑
Z	X→	Z	X→	Z	X→	Z	X→	Z
X↑	Y	X↑	Y	X↑	Y	X↑	Y	X↑
Z	X→	Z	X→	Z	X→	Z	X→	Z
X↑	Y	X↑	Y	X↑	Y	X↑	Y	X↑
Z	X→	Z	X→	Z	X→	Z	X→	Z
X↑	Y	X↑	Y	X↑	Y	X↑	Y	X↑

Setting Diagram

4. Cut 4 borders, ⅞" wide, from cream print. Join to quilt and miter corners.

5. Cut 4 borders, 2⅞" wide, from med. blue floral print. Join to quilt and miter corners.

6. Cut 4 borders, 1" wide, from blue. Join to quilt and miter corners.

7. Cut 4 borders, 1⅜" wide, from med. blue floral print. Join to quilt and miter corners.

Quilting
Quilt blocks as shown in Quilting Diagrams for each block. Outline-quilt outside seam line of cream

print border and outside seam lines of blue border. Sandra quilted a broken lattice strip design in her inner med. blue floral print border. Quilt a straight line down the center of outer med. blue floral print border.

Finished Edges
Bind with blue fabric.

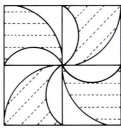

Block X

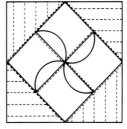

Block Y

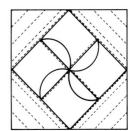

Block Z

Quilting Diagrams

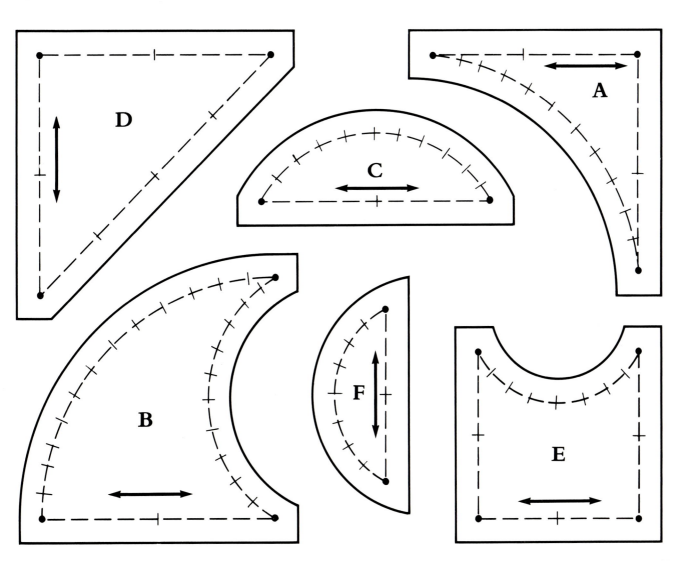

Pauline Warren

Sidney, Ohio

"One of the things that I like best about quilting," says Pauline, "is that I have something to show for the time I spend on it." Pauline is employed as a computer programmer, and she is reminded daily of the sharp contrast between programming and quilting. "Most of what I do as a programmer is intangible," she says. "I've never had anyone look at a printout and say, 'What a beautiful program!' "

Having done some form of needlework since she was a child, Pauline says that it seems as if she always knew how to quilt. But it was not until after her mother's death that she really invested more time in quilting. Her mother was a quilter and left Pauline with many unfinished quilts. As Pauline completed each one, her love for quilting grew. "I do wish that I had started quilting sooner," she says, "so that my mother and I could have shared time quilting."

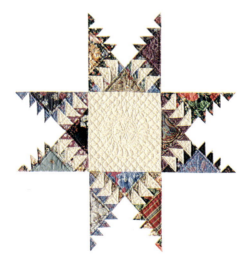

Delectable Mountain Star
1990

"This one is not for sale," says Pauline. "I put too much of myself into it." In an effort to get rid of her collection of scraps, Pauline sat down and pieced several Rising Sun blocks. "I thought I would just use these blocks to make a sample design," she says, "and then later I would remake them in other colors. But the more I worked on the design using the scrap fabrics, the better I liked it." After several weeks of arranging the setting, Pauline settled on the one you see here.

Beautifully quilted feathered wreaths with a crosshatched background enhance this magnificent scrap quilt.

Setting Diagram

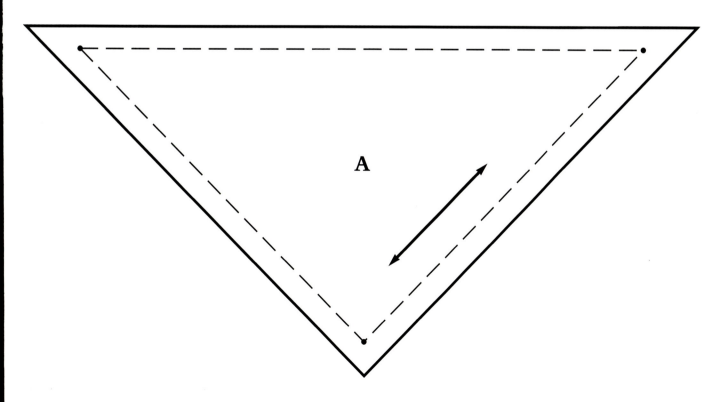

A

69

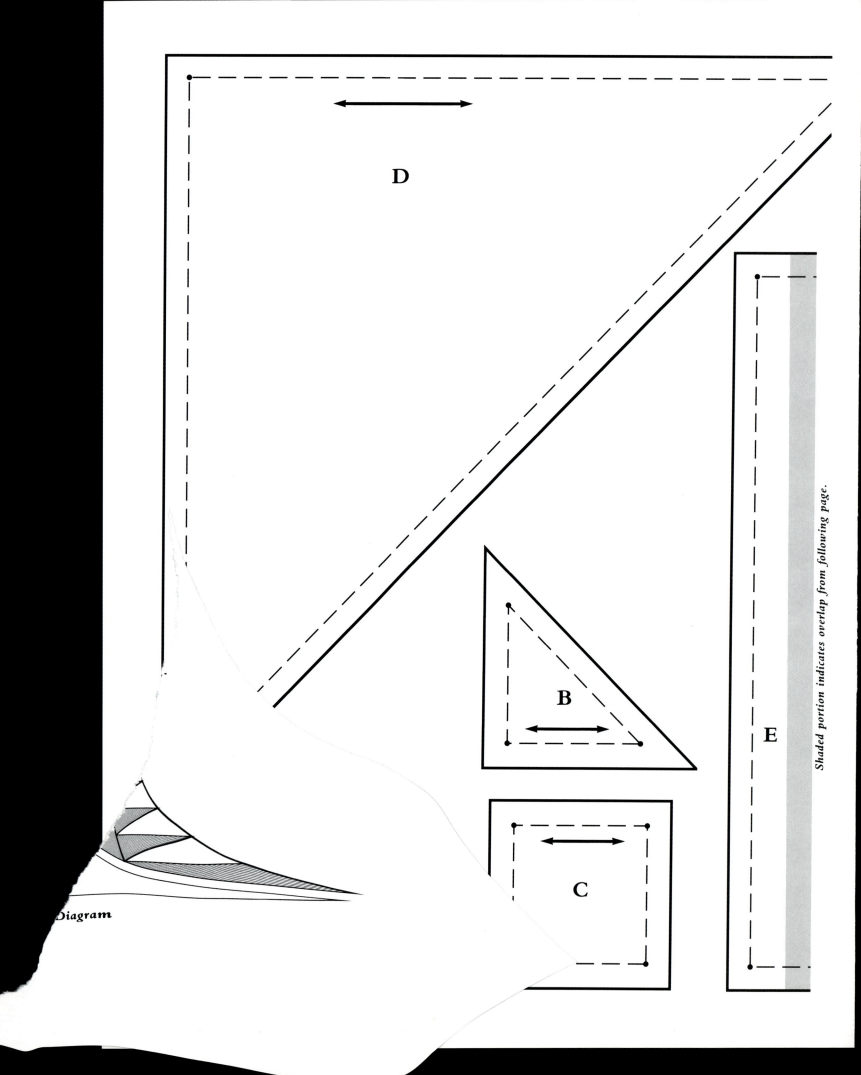

D

B

C

E

Diagram

Shaded portion indicates overlap from following page.

D

E

Swatches
1990

Don't toss out those swatches you receive from mail-order fabric stores. Round them up and stitch them together to make this jiffy wall hanging.

Pauline had accumulated so many swatches in the mail that it was becoming a problem. "I didn't want to throw them away," she says, "so I decided to use them in a quilt."

To her surprise, the quilt also turned out to be a study in color values. Since the quilt required numerous contrasting light and dark prints, Pauline used many fabrics more than once. For instance, a print could be used as the darker print in one block, and then the same print could be used again as the lighter print in another block. "It was interesting to see how the color values changed, depending on whether the print was used as a dark or light one," says Pauline.

72

Swatches

Finished Quilt Size
42″ x 42″

**Number of Blocks and
Finished Size**
100 blocks—3″ x 3″

Fabric Requirements
Dk. prints   —1 yd. total
Lt. prints   —1 yd. total
Dk. border
  print/stripe   —1¼ yd.
Rose print   —½ yd.
Print for
  binding   —½ yd.
Backing   —1½ yd.

Number to Cut
Square   —450 dk. prints
               450 lt. prints

Quilt Top Assembly
1. Alternate light and dark prints to make 50 each of blocks A and B, as shown in Block Piecing Diagrams.

Block A

Block B

Block Piecing Diagrams

2. Alternate 5 block As with 5 block Bs, beginning with a block A, and join at sides to form a row. Make 5 Block A rows.

Make 5 more rows (Block B rows), alternating blocks, but beginning with a block B.
3. Alternate rows, beginning with a Block A row, and join rows.
4. Cut 4 borders, 3½″ wide, from border print/stripe. Join to quilt and miter corners.
5. Cut 4 borders, 3½″ wide, from rose print. Join to quilt and miter corners.

Quilting
Quilt diagonally through the light print squares in both directions to form a cross-hatching pattern. Follow the design of the border print/stripe and quilt. Quilt a feather design with round corners on rose print border.

Finished Edges
Round off corners following curve of quilting design and bind with print fabric.

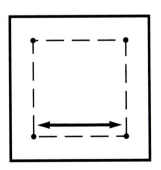

73

Kim Brooks

Lewiston, Idaho

When Kim's wife, Pam, asked for his help on a quilt she was making, little did he know that he would soon be joining the quilting ranks. "It was then that I discovered quilting's clean and quiet side," says Kim, "and the craft offered a large format that was perfect for my artwork."

Kim especially enjoys working on projects with Pam. "We have such fun developing new ideas and adding our own individual talents and tastes to a project," says Kim. Sharing a love for quilting has one drawback though, he says. "When we are working on different projects, it gets really crowded in the sewing room! It's hard to get a turn at the sewing machine."

Kim is also proficient in metalworking, woodworking, and pottery, but he finds quiltmaking the most amenable to his life as a husband, father, and student. He calls himself a "secondhand" member of Pam's quilting guild, Seaport Quilters' Guild.

Goin' Home
1989

Concern for planetary ecology was Kim's inspiration for this quilt. "I made this quilt to remind everyone of our vanishing sea turtles," says Kim. The red turtle is his way of warning us that the last turtle of the species may be alive right now.

Kim's turtles are in brush batik and layer-appliquéd to a solid background. If you have never tried to make a brush batik or feel a little uncomfortable with the process, try it on a small scale first. We suggest using the pattern pieces at the size printed, rather than enlarging them, and making a small wall hanging before leaping into a large project.

Batik wax and brushes can be purchased at your local art supply store or ordered from an art supply catalog.

Karen K. Buckley

Carlisle, Pennsylvania

"Since beginning to quilt in 1982," says Karen, "I have not stopped. The satisfaction I get from making a quilt is like no other." Karen's enthusiasm for quiltmaking motivated her to fulfill her dream of owning a quilt shop. "I started the business with 80 bolts of fabric and very few books and supplies," says Karen, "but when I closed the shop three years later, I had close to 1,000 bolts of fabric, more than 100 different books, and every sewing notion you could imagine."

The experience as a quilt shop owner was rewarding for Karen, not only financially, but also in teaching others and in seeing their projects completed. "Quilting has brought so many wonderful people and happenings into my life," says Karen, "that I can hardly wait to see what is in store for me next."

Joe's Quilt
1989

It all started when Karen's husband, Joe, commented that she had never made a quilt for him. "Of all the things you have quilted and given away," he said to Karen, "you never have made me a quilt." That was enough of a "quilt guilt trip" to start Karen sewing!

If the pattern for *Joe's Quilt* looks familiar, it is because it is taken from the *Morning Glory Lane* quilt, found in an issue of *Quiltmaker*. (See "Resources" for details.) Since Karen was in a hurry to complete a quilt for Joe, she developed a strip-piecing method to decrease assembly time. She also changed the colors (seen in the magazine) from feminine hues to more masculine ones.

By the way, Joe proudly displays his quilt on his office wall.

Joe's Quilt

Finished Quilt Size
45½″ x 45½″

Number of Blocks and Finished Size
9 blocks—10″ x 10″

Fabric Requirements
Teal	—½ yd.
Teal print	—½ yd.
Brown print	—1 yd.
Cream print	—1 yd.
Brown paisley print	—1¼ yd.
Brown paisley print for bias binding	—1 yd.
Backing	—2¾ yd.

Quilt Top Assembly
1. Cut 1 strip across the grain, 2¼″ wide, from teal. Cut 1 strip across the grain, 2¼″ wide, from teal print. Join strips lengthwise to form a panel, as shown in Block Piecing Diagram I. Cut 18 segments across panel seam line at 2¼″ intervals. Position segments to form checkerboard square, as shown in Block Piecing Diagram I. Make 9.

Block Piecing Diagram I

Cut 2 strips across the grain, 2¼″ wide, from brown print. Cut 18 segments (rectangles) at 4″ intervals. Join strips to opposite sides of checkerboard squares, as shown in Block Piecing Diagram II.

Block Piecing Diagram II

Cut 1 strip across the grain, 4″ wide, from brown print. Cut 1 strip each across the grain, 2¼″ wide, from teal and teal print. Join strips lengthwise, as shown in Block Piecing Diagram III. Cut 18 segments across panel seam lines at 2¼″ intervals. Join segments to opposite sides of block, rotating strips as shown in Block Piecing Diagram IV.

Block Piecing Diagram III

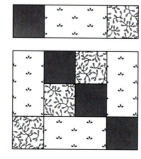

Block Piecing Diagram IV

Cut 3 strips across the grain, 5⅞″ wide, from cream print. Cut 18 segments (squares) at 5⅞″ intervals. Cut squares in half on the diagonal to form 36 triangles. Join triangles to 2 opposite sides of each block first. Then join triangles to remaining sides, as shown in Block Piecing Diagram V. Make 9 blocks.

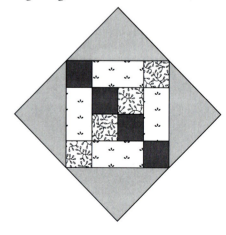

Block Piecing Diagram V

🔲 *brown print*   🔳 *cream print*

🔳 *teal print*   ⬛ *teal*

🔳 *brown paisley print*

82

2. Cut 4 strips across the grain, 2¼″ wide, from brown paisley print. Cut 72 segments (squares) at 2¼″ intervals.

Cut 6 strips across the grain, 2⅝″ wide, from brown print. Cut 96 segments (squares) at 2⅝″ intervals. Cut squares in half on the diagonal to form 192 triangles.

Cut 2 strips across the grain, 2⅝″ wide, from teal. Cut 32 segments (squares) at 2⅝″ intervals. Cut squares in half on the diagonal to form 64 triangles.

Join 3 squares with 10 triangles to form sashing, as shown in Sashing Piecing Diagram. Make 24. (You will have 16 teal triangles remaining. Set these aside.)

Sashing Diagram

3. Alternate 4 sashing strips with 3 blocks to form a block row, as shown in Setting Diagram I. Make 3 rows.

Cut 2 strips across the grain, 3″ wide, from cream print. Cut 16 segments (squares) at 3″ intervals.

Alternate 4 cream print squares with 3 sashing strips to form a sashing row, as shown in Setting Diagram I. Make 4 rows.

Join sashing rows to block rows.

4. Cut 4 strips across the grain, 1¾″ wide, from brown paisley print. Cut 12 segments at 1¾″ intervals. Trim ends of each segment at a 45° angle, as shown on Border Strip Diagram.

Trim.

Border Strip Diagram

Alternate 4 teal triangles with 3 strips, as shown in Setting Diagram II, and join to make a pieced border. Make 4 and set aside.

5. Cut 4 strips across the grain, 2″ wide, from brown paisley print. Cut each strip into 39¼″ segments. Trim ends at a 45° angle, as done for previous border. Join border strips to pieced border, as shown in Setting Diagram II. Join borders to quilt.

6. Cut 1 strip across the grain, 6⅜″ wide, from brown paisley print. Cut 2 segments (squares) at 6⅜″ intervals. Cut squares in half on the diagonal to make 4 triangles. Join triangles to corners of quilt, as shown in Setting Diagram II.

Quilting
Outline-quilt ¼″ inside seam line of all triangles and squares. Quilt a 1″ cross-hatching pattern in every cream print triangle.

Finished Edges
Bind with brown paisley print.

Setting Diagram I

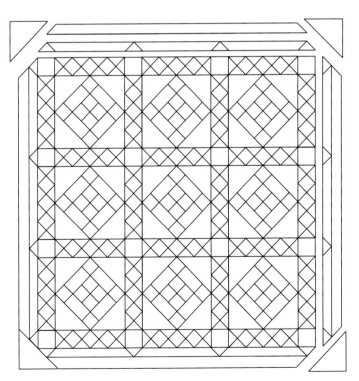

Setting Diagram II

Janet Phillips

Holdrege, Nebraska

Janet Phillips is the first quilter in her family. "Everyone in our family tree sewed, but there were no quilters!" she says. Nonetheless, as with many who learn to quilt, Janet has joined the ranks of the addicted-to-quilting set. "A group of us don't think twice about overnight fabric shopping trips, even out of state," she says, "or about long drives to conventions or meetings."

Janet finds that getting others excited about quilting is just as rewarding as quilting itself. She presents quilt lectures around Nebraska and teaches quilting at the local community college. In addition to spending 20 to 25 hours a week quilting, Janet plays an active role in her guild, The Prairie Quilt Guild, and served as president in 1990.

Though Janet loves quilting and does it well, she has no desire to become a professional. "I want to keep my quilting something that I want to do," says Janet, "and not a schedule that I have to keep."

Bear Crossing
1990

Much preliminary planning goes into making a successful quilt such as Janet's *Bear Crossing*. This elegant quilt is Janet's variation of the traditional pattern, Bear's Paw. One might even think of it as a paw-within-a-paw because of the repeated pattern.

Janet feels most comfortable with sketching a pattern on graph paper with colored pencils and making adjustments until the design becomes her own. Her use of silver metallic thread for quilting *Bear Crossing* is another reflection of her skill as a designer. She selected silver thread to coordinate with the silver in her floral print. Use of metallic thread in a quilt is successful if it enhances the overall design. As you can see, Janet's decision to use metallic thread for *Bear Crossing* was a correct one.

Bear Crossing

Finished Quilt Size
80" x 100"

**Number of Blocks and
Finished Size**
12 blocks—14" x 14"

Fabric Requirements
White-on-white
  print   —4 yd.★
Cream/blue print —½ yd.
Maroon print   —2½ yd.★
Pink/blue print★★ —1 yd.
Pink print   —2½ yd.
Slate blue print —1¾ yd.
Maroon print for
  bias binding —1¼ yd.
Backing   —5¾ yd.
★See steps 2 and 3 before cutting
fabrics.
★★This is a floral print with silver
accents.

Other Materials
Silver metallic thread

Number to Cut
Template A   —48 maroon print
         48 pink print
Template B   —108 white-on-white
         print
Template C   —48 cream/blue
         print
Template D   —96 pink/blue
         print
Template E   —96 pink print
         192 maroon print
Template F   —96 white-on-white
         print
         192 slate blue
         print
Template G   —48 white-on-white
         print
Template H   —48 pink print
Template H★★★ —48 pink print
Template I   —128 pink/blue
         print
         128 white-on-white
         print

Template J   —128 pink print
         128 slate blue
         print
Template K   —64 pink print
★★★Flip or turn over template if
fabric is one-sided.

Quilt Top Assembly
1. Join pieces A, B, D, E, and H to
make a unit, as shown in Block
Piecing Diagram I. Refer to color
photograph of block for proper
color placement. Make 48 units.

Block Piecing Diagram I

Join 4 units to pieces B and C, as
shown in Block Piecing Diagram II.
Make 12.

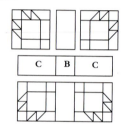

Block Piecing Diagram II

Join B, F, and G to form strips,
as shown in Block Piecing Diagram
III. Join strips to sides of blocks, as
shown.

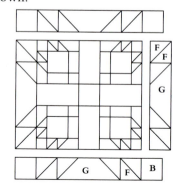

Block Piecing Diagram III

2. Cut six 14½″ squares from white-on-white print and set aside.

Cut five 14⅞″ squares from white-on-white print. Cut these squares in half on the diagonal to make 10 triangles and set aside.

Cut one 15¼″ square from white-on-white print. Finger-crease square in half on the diagonal; open square and finger-crease square in half on opposite diagonal. Cut square on finger-creased lines to make 4 triangles.

Alternate white-on-white pieces with Bear Crossing blocks (BCB), as shown in Setting Diagram and quilt photograph. Join pieces into rows and corner sections. Join rows and corner sections.

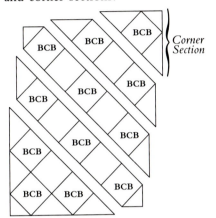

BCB = *Bear Crossing Block*

Setting Diagram

3. Cut 4 border strips, 1″ wide, from maroon print. (After adding this border strip, the quilt needs to measure 60″ x 80″. Vary the width of your border strip from the measurement given as needed in order to get this measurement.)

4. Join pieces I, J, and K, as shown in Border Block Piecing Diagram. (See quilt photograph for proper color placement.) Make 28 border blocks.

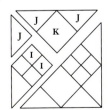

Border Block Piecing Diagram

Join pieces I, J, and K, as shown in Corner Border Block Piecing diagram. Make 4 corner border blocks.

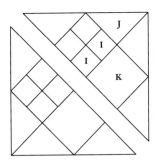

Corner Border Block Piecing

5. Join 8 border blocks at sides for side border. Make 2 borders. Join to opposite sides of quilt, as shown in quilt photograph.

Join 6 border blocks at sides for top border. Repeat for bottom border. Join a corner border block to each end of each border. Join borders to quilt.

Quilting
All of Janet's quilting is done with silver metallic thread. A modified fleur-de-lis pattern is quilted in each large white-on-white print square and triangle. Quilt blocks as shown in Block Quilting Diagram. The remainder of the area (shown in Setting Diagram) is quilted in 1″ parallel lines, running across the width of the quilt. Follow the seam lines of quilt border blocks and quilt-in-the-ditch, as shown in Border Block Quilting Diagram.

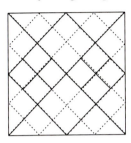

Border Block Quilting Diagram

Finished Edges
Bind with maroon print fabric.

Block Quilting Diagram

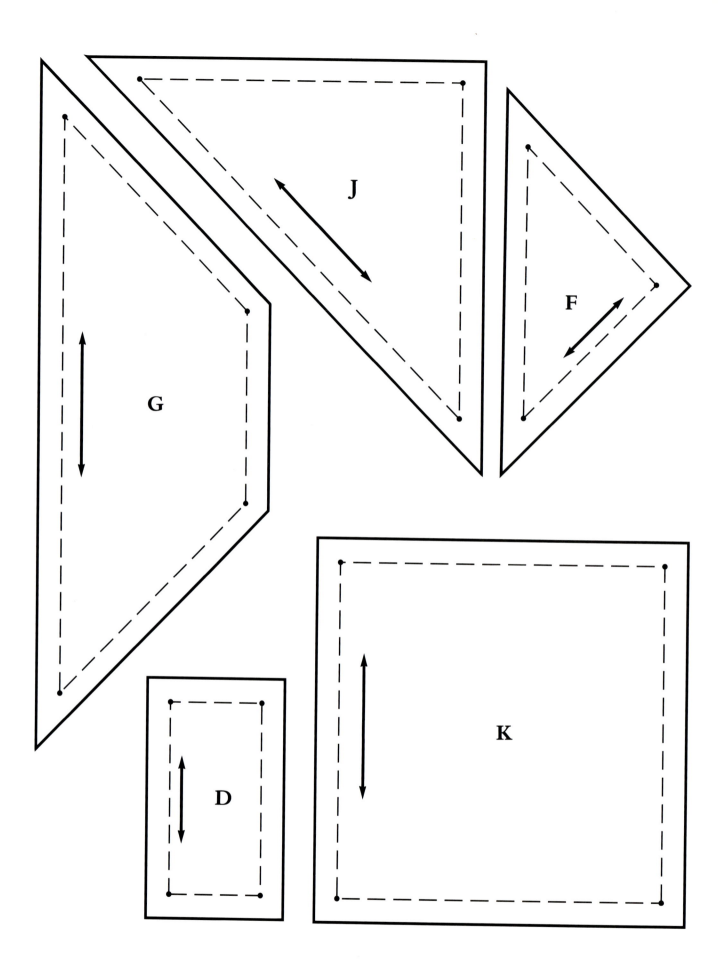

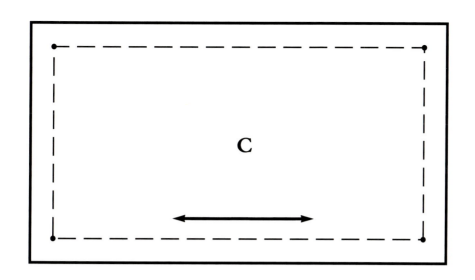

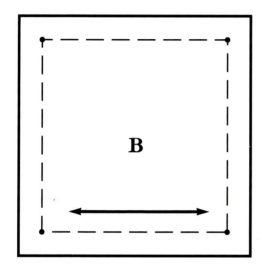

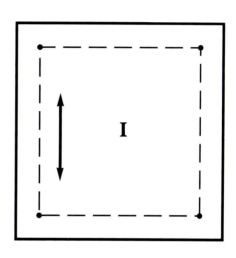

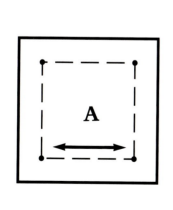

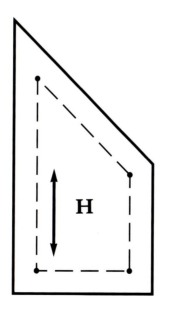

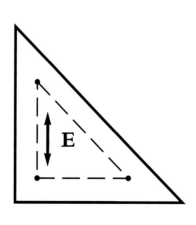

Marta Amundson
Riverton, Wyoming

As a professional quilter, Marta has become known as a maker of quilts with a message. Nineteen of her most recent works are a part of a series called Menagerie. "The goal of the series," she says, "is to stimulate people to think about their own lives and the environment around them."

Wide borders surrounding geometric patterns in solid brilliant colors are characteristic of her quilts. The wide borders provide ample space for her quilted silhouettes, which often relate to the quilt's theme. The solid colors and geometric shapes are reflective of her work as a stained glass artist. "I am grateful to the many teachers I had who instilled in me a sense of color and design that can be carried from one medium to another," says Marta.

When Pigs Have Wings
1990

Marta believes that humor is something that we each must grasp tightly in order to survive. So it is no surprise to find a quilt named *When Pigs Have Wings* in her Menagerie quilt series. "I designed this quilt to express those times when I just can't compromise anymore—when people have pushed me to my limit," she says, "and I make the decision to stand my ground until PIGS HAVE WINGS!"

Her patchwork design was inspired by an Amish quilt, *King's Cross Variation*, c. 1930. (See "Resources" for details.) *When Pigs Have Wings* uses quick-piecing techniques, which have become standard in her quilts. "I want every part of the quiltmaking process to be fun," says Marta.

When Pigs Have Wings

Finished Quilt Size
41½″ x 45½″

**Number of Blocks and
Finished Size**
42 blocks—4″ x 4″

Fabric Requirements
Solid colors   —1¼ yd. total
Lavender   —1 yd.★
Dk. green   —1½ yd.
Fuchsia for
   binding   —1⅜ yd.★
Backing   —1½ yd.
★If cutting strips for borders and
binding across the grain, only ¼
yard is required. See step 4 and
Finished Edges.

Other Materials
Freezer paper

Number to Cut
Triangle   —84 solid colors

Quilt Top Assembly
1. Cut 3½″-wide strips from solid
colors. Stack four strips and place
triangle template on strips, as
shown in Template Cutting Diagram. Cut fabric with a rotary
cutter.

Template Cutting Diagram

2. Cut 1½″-wide strips from solid
colors. Join triangles to 1½″-wide
strips, as shown in Block Piecing
Diagram, varying color combinations. (See quilt photograph.)

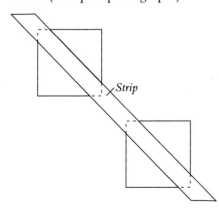

Block Piecing Diagram

Marta suggests string-piecing triangles to strips to save time, but be
sure to leave enough space between

triangles so that there is ample fabric available to make the corners of the blocks. (See Block Piecing Diagram.) Press blocks, place 4½″ square template on blocks, and trim edges to square off block.

3. Arrange blocks in 7 rows of 6 blocks each so that the diagonal bars form Xs. (See quilt photograph.) Before joining blocks, make sure you are pleased with the color arrangement. Join blocks at sides to form rows and then join rows.

4. Cut 2 border strips, 1¼″ wide, from lavender and join to top and bottom of quilt.

Cut 2 border strips, 1¼″ wide, from lavender and join to sides of quilt.

5. Cut 2 borders, 8½″ wide, from dk. green and join to sides of quilt.

Cut 2 borders, 8½″ wide, from dk. green and join to top and bottom of quilt.

Quilting

Marta coordinated colored quilting thread with the colors of her fabrics. Outline-quilt outside seam lines of all diagonal bars and lavender border strip. Duplicate the *X* pattern, formed by the pieced blocks, by quilting across adjoining blocks, as shown in Quilting Diagram.

Make a pigs-with-wings quilting template from freezer paper. Stack 6 sheets of freezer paper and place quilting pattern on top. Press the freezer paper edges together with a warm iron to keep the sheets from moving while you cut around the outline. Place the cutouts on the quilt border to determine the spacing that you want and press them in place. Trace the pattern and peel off the templates. Repeat for the remainder of the border. (Freezer paper templates can be reused.)

Finished Edges

Bind with fuchsia fabric.

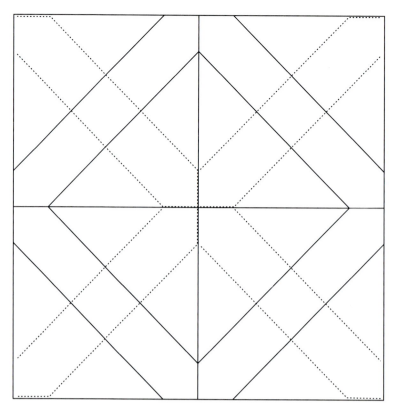

Quilting Diagram

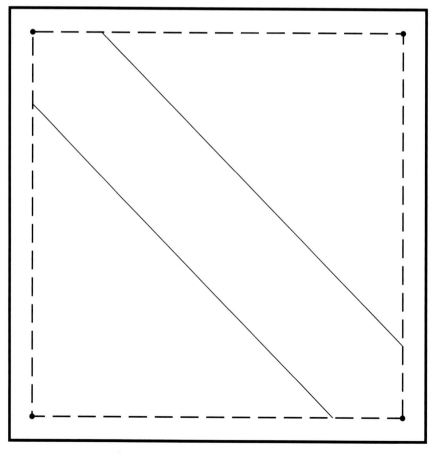

Template for Trimming Blocks

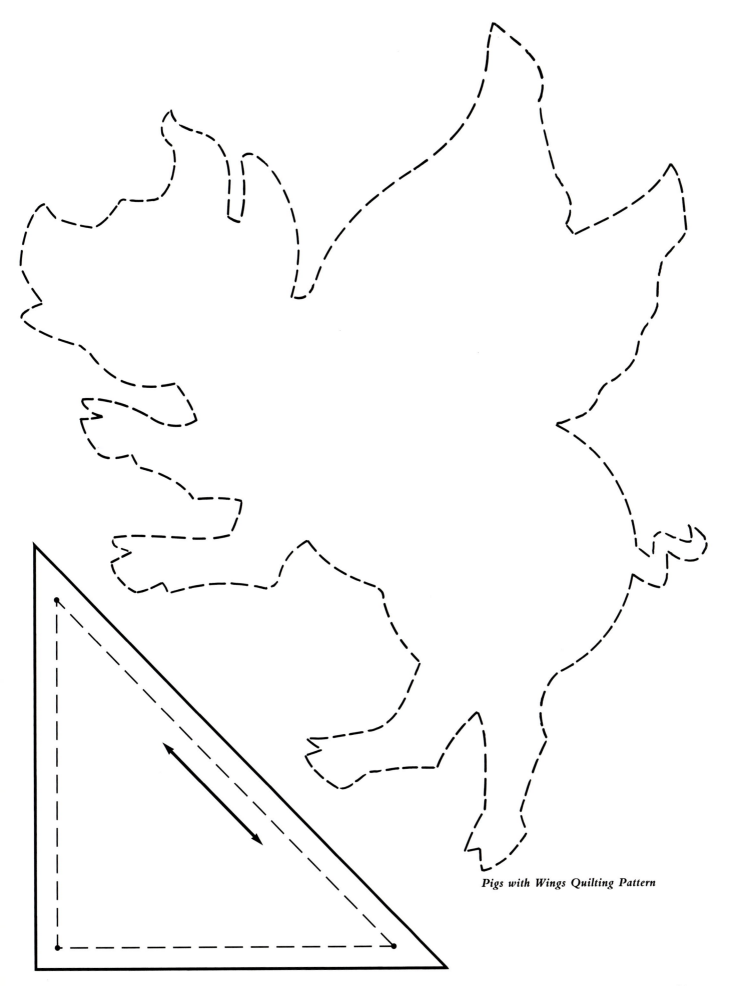

Pigs with Wings Quilting Pattern

93

Linda Lewis

Kailua, Hawaii

The best parts of quiltmaking, according to Linda, are giving quilts away and sharing the craft with others. Four years ago she developed a quilting project for elementary school children, and, says Linda, "I'm still getting feedback! Many children are working on projects of their own. Others ask me when we are going to do it again."

Linda loves to combine mediums—in this case painting on fabric and quiltmaking. She does all of her quilts, the majority of which are wall hangings, this way. She paints so well on fabric that people frequently ask her where she bought the printed fabric. "I love to paint," says Linda, "but I don't draw as well as I'd like. By painting some portion of the quilt, I can still express myself with a paintbrush."

Linda is a member of the Hawaii Quilt Guild and the Hawaii Stitchery and Fiber Arts Guild.

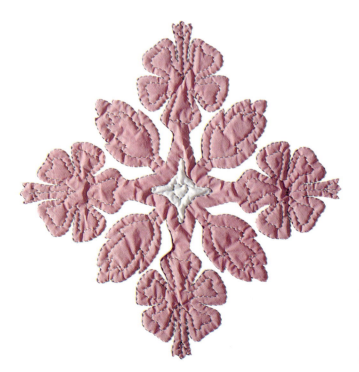

Pua'aloalo Lei
1990

If you can't go to Hawaii, try the next best thing—put a touch of it in your home. The clean, fresh look of Linda's *Pua'aloalo Lei* can be a year-round reminder of the satiny beaches and balmy breezes.

Pua'aloalo lei is Hawaiian for "hibiscus flower lei." Linda began with a floral print, which inspired her to make a hibiscus medallion. She found a hibiscus pattern in Elizabeth Root's *Hawaiian Quilting* (see "Resources") and painted it on fabric. She continued the theme by quilting a hibiscus lei along the borders.

As with most Hawaiian quilt patterns, no two designs are alike; therefore, we created our own hibiscus pattern for your use, or you can create one of your own in the true Hawaiian quilting tradition. Linda uses a low-loft batting.

Pua'aloalo Lei

Finished Quilt Size
36" x 36"

Fabric Requirements
White★ —1 yd.
White —1 yd.
Floral print —1¼ yd.★★
Pink —¼ yd.
Backing —1¼ yd.

★Use a 50/50 polyester/cotton blend for fabric painting.
★★Includes yardage for binding.

Other Materials
Fabric eraser
Fabric paint, pink
Fabric paintbrush
Iron
Quilting thread, white, black, gray, and pink
Tape, transparent
Thread, black pearl cotton #8 or similar thread
Wax paper

Quilt Top Assembly
1. On a small scrap of white polyester/cotton fabric, apply paint to test for feathering or bleeding. (If feathering occurs, select another fabric.) Cut a 21" square from white polyester/cotton blend. Make a template of hibiscus design. Center and trace design on fabric square with pencil. Also, sketch in lines inside design. (See photograph of painted hibiscus.)

Before painting, tape fabric to wax paper to anchor it while you paint and to keep fabric from being soiled. Paint up to, but not over pencil lines, except those on outside edges of the design. There will be white areas left inside the motif. Set paint according to the directions of your fabric paint. (These are general instructions, so be sure to follow directions for the paint you purchase.)

2. Trim painted square to a 20⅜" square. Cut two 14⅞" squares from floral print. Cut each in half on the diagonal to make 4 triangles. Join triangles to sides of square.

3. Cut 4 borders, 4½" wide, from white cotton. Join borders to 2 opposite sides of quilt.

Cut four 4½" squares from pink. Join squares to each end of 2 remaining borders. Join borders to opposite sides of quilt.

Quilting
Using black thread and large stitches (similar to Japanese Sashiko stitching), outline-quilt the hibiscus design. Follow pencil lines for quilting hibiscus interior, as shown in close-up photograph of hibiscus. Quilt a heart in the center. Quilt in-the-ditch of painted square seam line. With white quilting thread, echo-quilt hibiscus design to fill the remainder of the center square.

With gray quilting thread, quilt parallel lines, 1" apart, in floral print triangles. With pink quilting thread, quilt Linda's hibiscus lei pattern along borders. Quilt a hibiscus in each pink square with gray quilting thread.

Finished Edges
Bind with floral print.

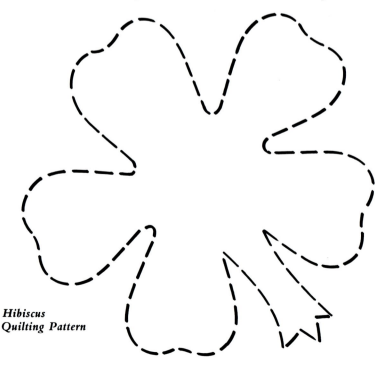

Hibiscus Quilting Pattern

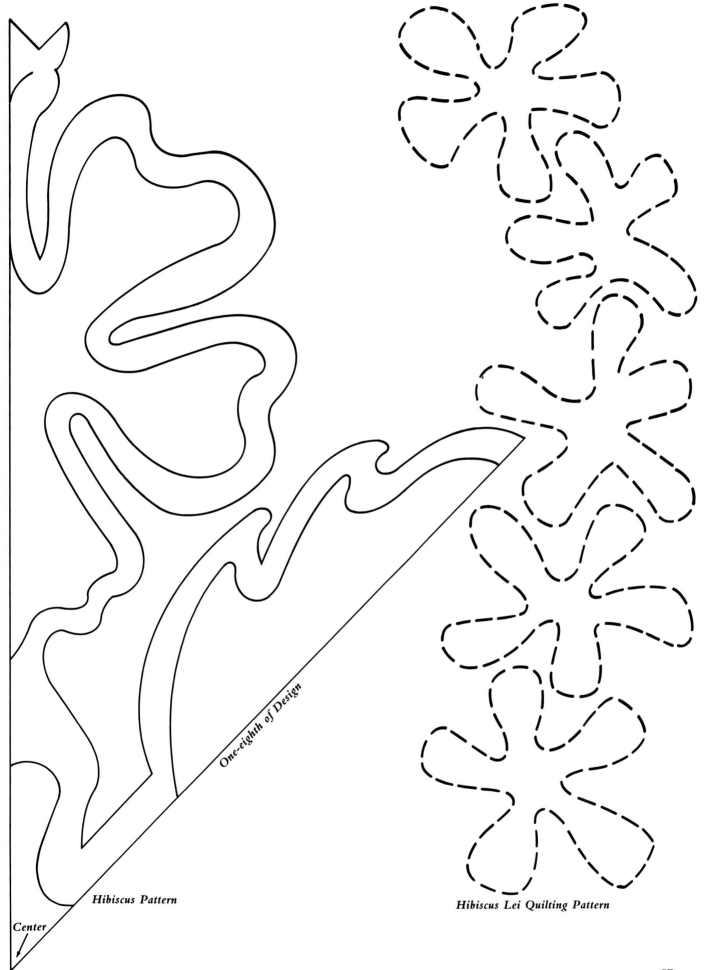

One-eighth of Design

Hibiscus Pattern

Center

Hibiscus Lei Quilting Pattern

Linda's Hand-Painted Quilted Ornaments
1990 and 1991

If you get cold feet when thinking about fabric painting and quiltmaking, here's a way to eliminate your hypothermia. Linda's ornaments average 4″ square. (They are more fun when you can use your scraps to make them.) Experiment with fabric and paint colors on the designs here or design your own pattern. Try making a few to match your kitchen wallpaper or to repeat a pattern in your favorite quilt. But, quilter, beware—betcha can't make just one!

Linda's Hand-Painted Quilted Ornaments

Materials Required
Batting, low loft
Fabric for backing
Fabric, white or light unbleached polyester/cotton blend for fabric painting
Fabric eraser
Fabric paintbrushes
Fabric paints
Felt-tip marking pen, medium point
Iron
Needle, embroidery
Paper, white drawing
Ring, small plastic for hanging
Ruler
Tape, transparent
Thread, black pearl cotton #8 or embroidery floss
Wax paper

Ornament Assembly
1. Draw desired block design (preferably a square) with a pencil on drawing paper. Add ½″ margin outside block (square). With felt-tip pen, retrace all pencil lines to darken them.

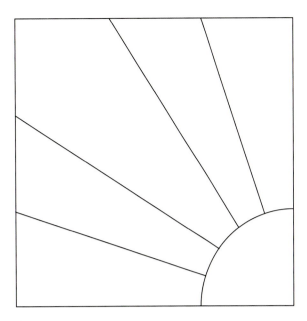

Sunrise

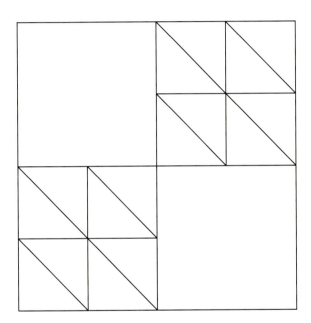

Flock of Geese

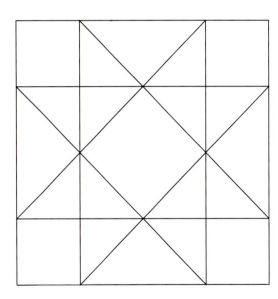

Variable Star

2. Cut a square at least ½″ larger than your drawing from fabric. Place fabric over drawing and trace design and ½″ margin line on fabric with a pencil.

3. Tape fabric square to wax paper to anchor it while you paint and to keep fabric from being soiled. Paint up to, but not over pencil lines.

Add pindots by using point of paintbrush, if desired. Set paint according to the directions of your fabric paint. (These are general instructions, so be sure to follow directions for the paint you purchase.)

4. After paint has set, assemble ornament for quilting. Cut batting a little larger than painted fabric. Cut backing with a 1″ margin. Layer painted top, batting, and backing. Pin or baste layers together to stabilize while quilting.

5. Using black thread, quilt along pencil lines with large Japanese Sashiko-like stitches, as shown.

6. Trim painted fabric and batting to ½″ margin line. Trim backing ⅝″ wider than top and batting.

7. Fold backing over top to form a ⁵⁄₁₆″-wide binding. Pin and blind-stitch to top. Attach small ring to top left corner or top center. Sign and date ornament.

Beverley Cosby
Mechanicsville, Virginia

"It's the doing rather than the having that gives me the most plea-sure in quiltmaking," says Beverley. "I enjoy the time that I spend piecing and quilting even more than having the actual finished quilt."

Beverley confesses that she was a little shy at first about entering her quilts in competitions. "Without the encouragement of my fel-low guild members, the Piecemakers [see page 134]," she says, "I don't believe I would ever have entered a contest." Since her first competition, she has won over 30 ribbons in local and national shows.

Her favorite method for learning new quiltmaking techniques is through books. "With a book," says Beverley, "I have the best teachers right with me at home, and I can work at my own pace."

Frank's Star
1987
Superbly pieced and quilted, *Frank's Star* was made by Beverley in honor of her father. "He loved the holidays," she says, "and the red, green, and white fabrics in this quilt reminded me of Christmas and, thus, of him."

Frank's Star has won several blue ribbons, including first place in the Traditional Pieced Quilts, Amateur category at the 5th Annual Ameri-can Quilter's Society Show, Padu-cah, Kentucky, in 1989; it also appeared in the '90 American Quilter's Society Calendar. (See "Resources.")

With more than 15 years of expe-rience as a quilter, Beverley has learned, through a process of trial and error, numerous sewing tech-niques to make quiltmaking more efficient and easier. Here are two of them: 1) To determine the correct length to cut borders, measure the width and length of the quilt top at the center rather than at the outside edges. This measurement will be more accurate than the one obtained by measuring the outside edges. 2) When joining multiple borders to a quilt, join the borders to each other first and then join the assem-bled borders to the quilt top. Both of these techniques will work espe-cially well with *Frank's Star*.

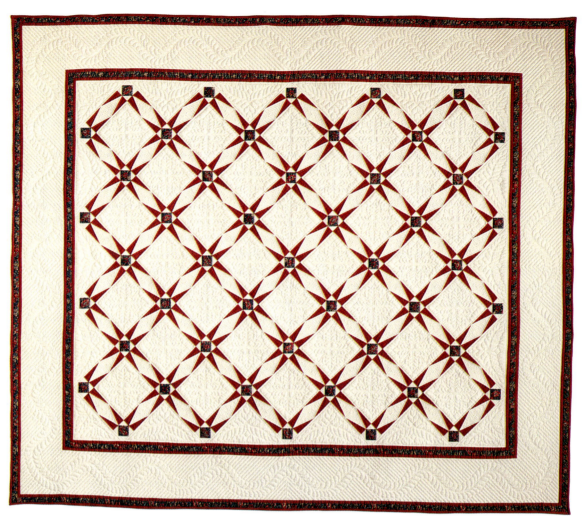

Frank's Star

Finished Quilt Size
88½″ x 104″

Fabric Requirements
Muslin	— 7¾ yd.
Maroon	— 3¼ yd.
Floral print	— 3¼ yd.
Maroon for bias binding	— 1¼ yd.
Backing	— 8⅞ yd.

Number to Cut★
Template A	— 49 floral print
Template B	— 196 muslin
Template C	— 160 maroon
Template C★★	— 160 maroon
Template D	— 80 muslin
Template E	— 32 muslin
Template F	— 4 muslin
Template G	— 14 muslin

★See steps 4 through 9 before cutting fabrics.

★★Flip or turn over template if fabric is one-sided.

Quilt Top Assembly

1. Join all triangles (B) to the sides of squares (A) to make unit 1s, as shown in Units Piecing Diagram. Make 49 unit 1s.

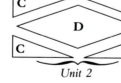

Unit 1   Unit 2

Units Piecing Diagram

Join all triangles (C) to the sides of diamonds (D) to make unit 2s, as shown in Units Piecing Diagram. Make 80 unit 2s.

2. Alternate unit 2s with squares (E), as shown in Setting Diagram I, and join at sides to form block rows.

Alternate unit 2s with unit 1s, as shown in Setting Diagram I, and join to form strip rows.

Make 2 corner sections, as shown.

3. Join block rows to strip rows, as shown in Setting Diagrams. Join triangles (G) to ends of all rows, as shown. Join rows to corner sections, as shown in Setting Diagram II.

4. Cut 4 borders, 1″ wide, from maroon. Join to quilt and miter corners.

Optional method: Join all borders, mentioned in steps 4 through 9, to each other before joining to quilt top. Mitering will be done with one long seam.

5. Cut 4 borders, 1½″ wide, from floral print. Join to quilt and miter corners.

6. Cut 4 borders, 1″ wide, from maroon. Join to quilt and miter corners.

7. Cut 4 borders, 8″ wide, from muslin. Join to quilt and miter corners.

8. Cut 4 borders, 1″ wide, from maroon. Join to quilt and miter corners.

9. Cut 4 borders, 1½″ wide, from floral print. Join to quilt and miter corners.

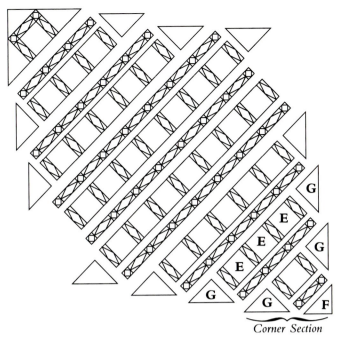

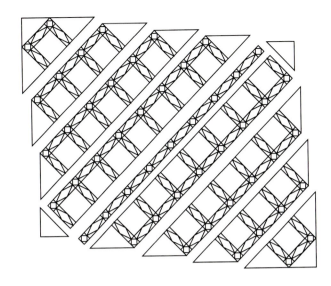

Corner Section

Setting Diagram I

Setting Diagram II

Quilting
Echo-quilt outside seam lines of square A, with lines ¼″ apart. Out-line-quilt ¼″ inside seam lines of triangles (C). Echo-quilt inside seam lines of diamonds (D), with lines ¼″ apart. Beverley quilted a snowflake pattern in squares (E). Feathers are quilted in triangles (F, G).

Outline-quilt outside seam lines of maroon borders. Quilt a running feather pattern in muslin borders. Background-quilt the remainder of borders with diagonal parallel lines, ½″ apart.

Finished Edges
Bind with maroon fabric.

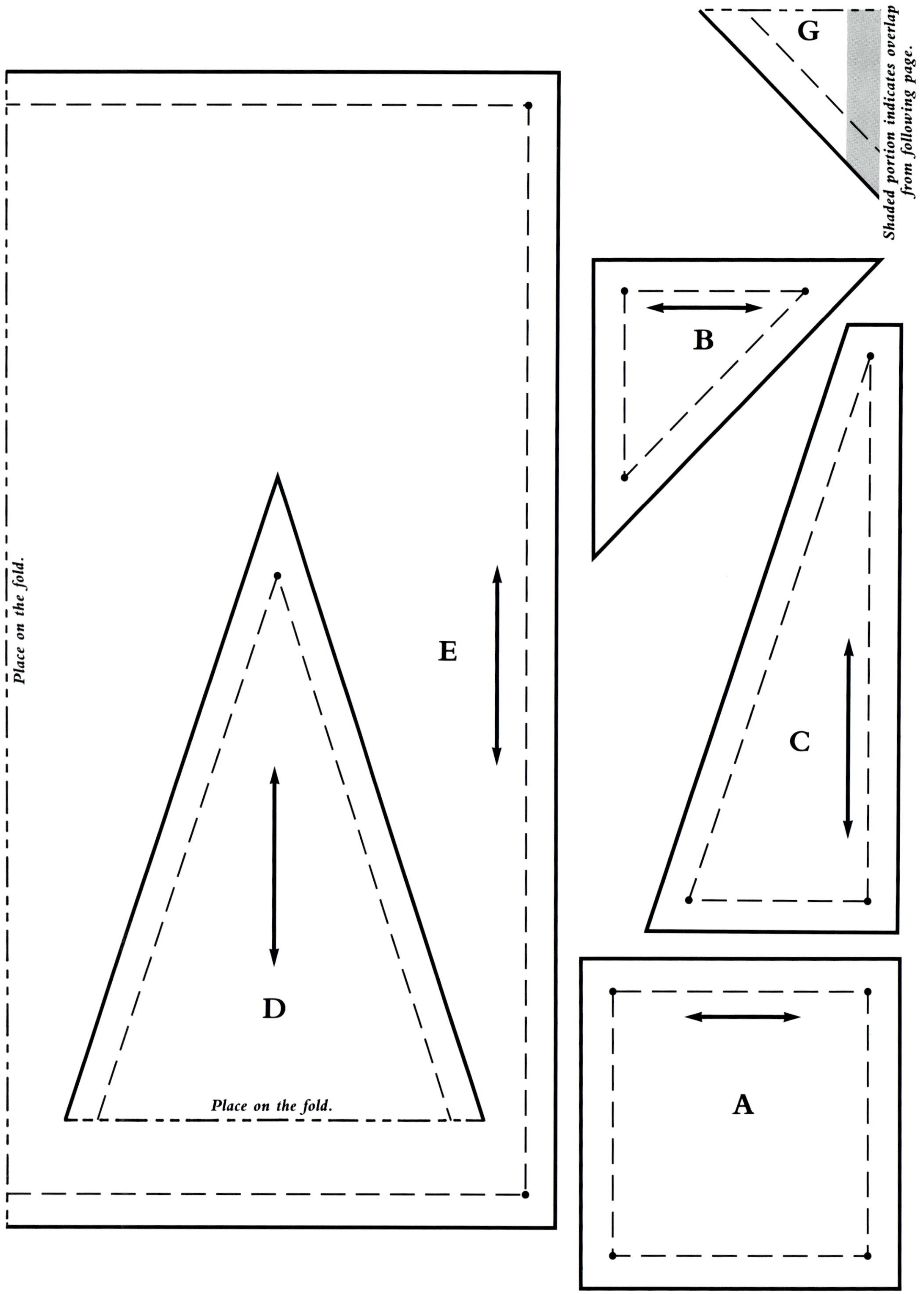

Place on the fold.

E

D

Place on the fold.

B

C

A

G

Shaded portion indicates overlap from following page.

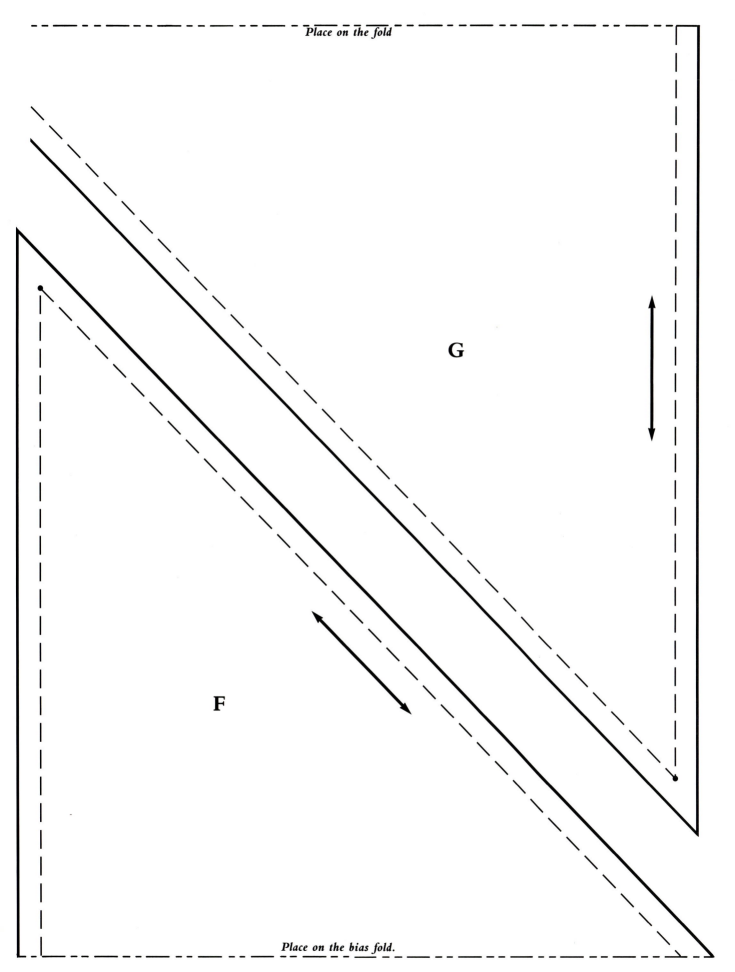

Place on the fold

G

F

Place on the bias fold.

105

TRADITIONS
IN
QUILTING

Rosie Stenger

Fort Madison, Iowa

Hours of quilting filled each day of Rosie Stenger's life. It was important to her to fulfill her goal of making one quilt for each of her 34 grandchildren. Before she died, she did just that, besides completing one for each of her seven children, a few more for relatives, five for the annual church harvest festival, and several for friends.

One of those grandchildren is Monica Bollin, who lives in Illinois and has the same dedication to and love of quilting her grandmother did. Monica, who has made several prize-winning quilts, today specializes in making quilt tops for sale. She is known to have pieced as many as nine quilt tops in a month. "My grandmother made beautiful quilts," says Monica, "and I suppose I got the 'disease' from her!"

Monica Bollin
Nauvoo, Illinois

Monica inherited all of Rosie's quilt patterns. "In essence, with these patterns, I have every quilt my grandmother ever made," says Monica. "It's like experiencing a part of her life."

Dresden Plate
1950s

Rosie's interpretation of the traditional Dresden Plate pattern is just as bright and cheerful as her name. It is a refreshing break from the numerous pastel renditions we have seen of this pattern.

This quilt belongs to Monica, her granddaughter, but Rosie never intended that Monica own it. It seems that although Rosie made many quilts, each grandchild was allowed to have only one, no more. And she was very firm when she said that she would not sell any of her other quilts to the family. Monica, however, felt she just *must* have this one. Since her grandmother was not against selling her quilts to people outside the family, Monica persuaded a neighbor to buy the quilt from Rosie and then sell it to *her*. Thus, Monica became the owner of *Dresden Plate*. Monica admits the way she got the quilt was sneaky, but she says she doubts that her grandmother was fooled.

Dresden Plate

Finished Quilt Size
77″ x 105½″

Number of Blocks and Finished Size
24 blocks—15⅝″ x 15⅝″

Fabric Requirements
Yellow — 1¾ yd.
White — 5⅝ yd.
Scraps — 5½ yd.
White for
  bias binding — 1½ yd.
Backing — 6¼ yd.

Number to Cut
Template A — 24 yellow
Template B — 432 scraps
Template C — 35 white
Template D — 2 scraps
Template D★ — 2 scraps
Template E — 91 scraps
Template F — 88 white
Template G — 1 white
Template G★ — 1 white
★Flip or turn over template if fabric is one-sided.

Quilt Top Assembly
1. Join 18 wedges (B) at sides to form a scalloped circle, as shown in Plate Piecing Diagram. Join wedges in half circles (9 wedges), sewing toward center from *seam line* (rather than from fabric edge). Join half circles to complete plate. Make 24 plates.

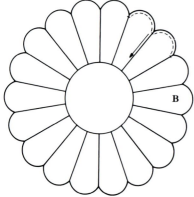

Plate Piecing Diagram

2. Cut twenty-four 16⅛″ squares from white. Finger-crease squares in half twice to find the center. Position plate in the center of each block and appliqué plate along scalloped edge. Baste inside circle of wedges to block to anchor plate in place. Appliqué circle (A) to center of plate. (See quilt drawing.) Trim

excess fabric from behind plate, leaving ¼″ seam allowance. Repeat for all 24 blocks.
   Optional method: Appliqué circle (A) to plate before appliquéing plate to block. After appliquéing plate to block, trim excess fabric from behind plate, leaving ¼″ seam allowance.
3. Cut 58 sashing strips, 1½″ x 16⅛″, from yellow. Alternate 5 sashing strips with 4 blocks and join to form a block row, as shown in Setting Diagram. Make 6 rows.
   Alternate 5 squares (C) with 4 sashing strips to form a sashing row, as shown in Setting Diagram. Make 7 sashing rows.
   Alternate sashing rows with block rows and join, as shown in Setting Diagram and quilt drawing.

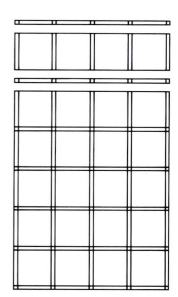

Setting Diagram

4. Alternate 34 wedges (E) with 33 triangles (F), twice, and join to make side borders. (See quilt drawing.) Join triangle (G) to one end and wedge (D) to the opposite end of each border, as shown in quilt drawing.

Alternate 23 wedges (E) with 22 triangles (F) and join to make bottom border, as shown in quilt drawing. Join wedges (D) to opposite ends of border.

Join side borders to quilt first and then bottom border. (See Border Corner Piecing Diagram.)

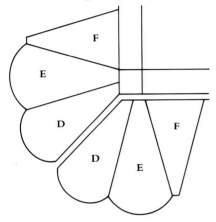

Border Corner Piecing Diagram

Quilting
Outline-quilt ¼″ inside seam lines of all wedges (B, D, E) and triangles (F, G). Outline-quilt ¼″ outside seam line of scalloped edge of plate and inside seam lines of all sashing. The circle (A) of each plate is quilted in a 1″ grid.

Finished Edges
With right sides together, sew a continuous bias strip for binding to quilt top along scalloped edge. Ease bias strip on the curves and pivot at seam lines between scallops. Miter or tuck binding at pivot points. Turn binding to back and blind-stitch in place.

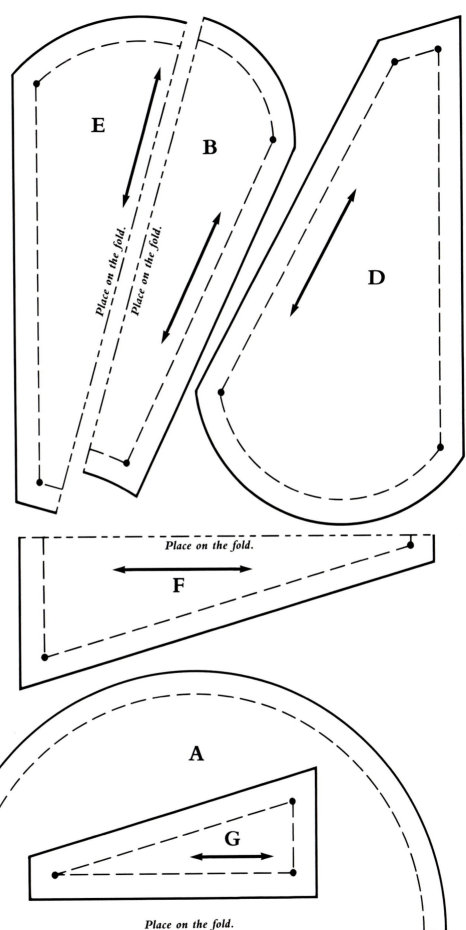

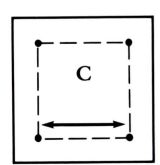

Anna Hartzell

Fremont, Michigan

Frequently, neighbors dropped in to visit Anna Hartzell when she was quilting. She was known for her quilting and her wonderful coffee. One visit by a young teenager named Milly Splitstone and her aunt proved to be a most special occasion. Anna was working on her *Autumn Leaves* quilt on that day, and Milly was immediately taken by the beauty of it. It was the first quilt with hand stitching that she had ever seen.

The impressions made on Milly that day inspired her to try quilting several years later. Today, she is also a quilt teacher and judge. In 1976, Milly was thrilled to have the opportunity to buy *Autumn Leaves* from a neighbor who cared for Anna in her last years. "People seldom have a chance to own the first quilt they ever saw," says Milly.

Autumn Leaves
1934–1935

The popularity of the Autumn Leaves pattern increased when it was seen at the Chicago World's Fair in 1933 at a quilt competition sponsored by Sears, Roebuck and Company. The pattern was readily available commercially in the 1930s and 1940s, so we suspect that this particular quilt was made from a commercial pattern. Nevertheless, the pattern's simplicity and beauty have held the admiration of quilters ever since.

Accurate vine and leaf placement can best be achieved by pinning all pieces in place before appliquéing. Instructions are written as Anna Hartzell made the quilt in the 1930s, but any one of the contemporary appliqué techniques is certainly suitable.

Autumn Leaves

Finished Quilt Size
82″ x 89″

Fabric Requirements
Prints	—3¼ yd. total
Pink	—2 yd.
Green	—1¼ yd.★
Muslin	—4½ yd.
Pink for bias binding	—1¼ yd.
Backing	—7⅝ yd.

★Approximately 35 yards of ¼″-wide (finished width measurement) bias binding are needed for vine and stems.

Number to Cut
Leaf	—634 prints

Quilt Top Assembly
1. Cut a 25″ x 32″ rectangle from muslin for center. Arrange vines, stems, and leaves on rectangle, as shown in quilt photograph and Setting Diagram. Pin in place and appliqué.

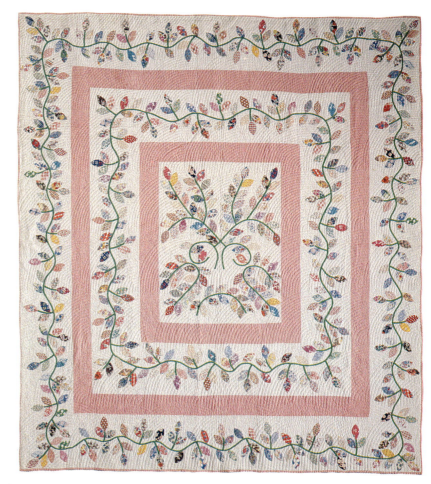

Setting Diagram

2. Cut 2 borders, 4½″ wide, from pink and join to top and bottom of quilt. Cut 2 borders, 4½″ wide, from pink and join to sides of quilt.
3. Cut 2 borders, 10½″ wide, from muslin and join to top and bottom of quilt. Cut 2 borders, 10½″ wide, from muslin and join to sides of quilt. Pin vine, stems, and leaves on muslin, as shown in quilt photograph, and appliqué.
4. Cut 2 borders, 4½″ wide, from pink and join to top and bottom of quilt. Cut 2 borders, 4½″ wide, from pink and join to sides of quilt.
5. Cut 2 borders, 11¼″ wide, from muslin and join to top and bottom of quilt. Cut 2 borders, 11¼″ wide, from muslin and join to sides of quilt. Pin vine, stems, and leaves on muslin, as shown in quilt photograph, and appliqué. (Appliquéing can also be done before joining borders to quilt.)

Quilting
Anna quilted an overall clamshell pattern on the entire quilt.

Finished Edges
Bind with pink fabric.

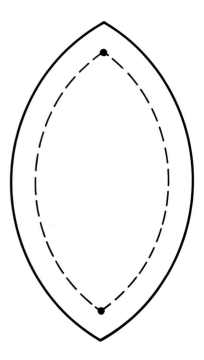

Jessie Krueger came from generations of quilters and left a quilting legacy for her children and grandchildren. Her daughter, Chrystal Sinn, has a headful of memories of sitting beside her mother at the quilting frame. Chrystal was the only one of Jessie's four children who followed in her mother's quilting footsteps, and Jessie encouraged her to quilt as soon as she was old enough to hold a needle. "I grew up watching how much my mother, grandmother, great-grandmother, and aunts loved and enjoyed quilting," says Chrystal. "And quilting has been a source of great pleasure to me all of my life, just as it was to them."

Jessie M. Krueger
Minier, Illinois

Pennsylvania Tulip
Pieced 1932
Quilted 1979

Chrystal Sinn
Minier, Illinois

A bit of Illinois was sent to young Chrystal Krueger (Sinn) in Pennsylvania in the form of a handsome quilt top, appropriately named *Pennsylvania Tulip*. Chrystal had moved

to begin her career as a teacher. To lessen Chrystal's anxiety at being away from home and to remind her of the family who loved and missed her, Jessie sent her something that she knew Chrystal would cherish, a patchwork top of pink tulips. "That is just the type of person my mother was—very loving," Chrystal says.

Chrystal stored the top in a cedar chest for many years, because time

to quilt became less and less frequent. Forty years later, when she pulled her mother's quilt top out of storage, she did what she thought was the most sensible thing at that time: She had the top quilted by a group of local quilters. Chrystal has since retired from teaching and is grateful to her mother for introducing her to quilting. "I now have this wonderful hobby to fill my days," says Chrystal.

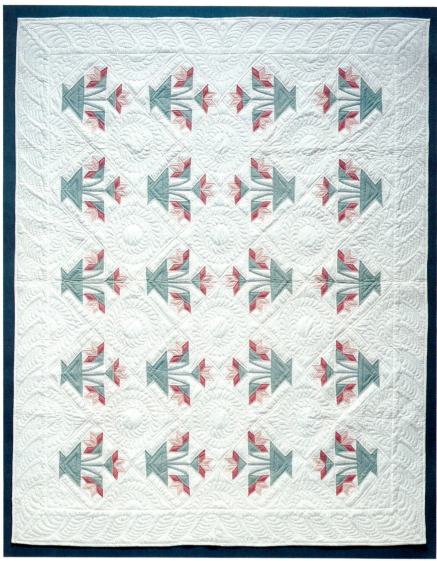

centers, as shown. Join triangle (D) to base. Join muslin triangles (B) and square (C) for middle tulip. Join muslin triangles (B, G) and square (F) for remaining tulips, as shown in Block Piecing Diagram I.

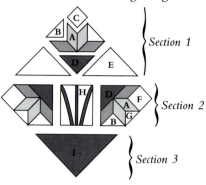

□ *pink*
▦ *dk. pink*
■ *green*

Block Piecing Diagram I

Join triangles (E) to sides of middle tulip to complete section 1, as shown. Appliqué stems (M, N) to rectangle (H), as shown. (Jesse top-stitched her stems to rectangle.) Join tulips to opposite sides of rectangle (H) to complete section 2, as shown. Join sections 1 through 3.

Join triangles (K) to the ends of rectangles (J), as shown in Block Piecing Diagram II. Join pieces to sides of block, as shown. Join triangle (L) to complete block. Make 20 blocks.

Block Piecing Diagram II

Pennsylvania Tulip

Finished Quilt Size
74″ x 90″

Number of Blocks and Finished Size
20 blocks—11″ x 11″

Fabric Requirements
Muslin, bleached	—6⅜ yd.
Pink	—¾ yd.
Dk. pink	—¾ yd.
Green	—1⅜ yd.
Muslin for bias binding	—1¼ yd.
Backing	—5½ yd.

Number to Cut
Template A	—60 pink
	60 dk. pink
Template A★	—60 pink
	60 dk. pink
Template B	—80 muslin★★
Template C	—20 muslin★★
Template D	—60 green
Template E	—40 muslin★★
Template F	—40 muslin★★
Template G	—40 muslin★★
Template H	—20 muslin★★
Template I	—20 green
Template J	—40 muslin★★
Template K	—40 green
Template L	—20 muslin★★
Template M	—20 green
Template N	—20 green
Template N★	—20 green
Template O	—14 muslin★★
Template P	—4 muslin★★
11½″ squares	—12 muslin★★

★Flip or turn over template if fabric is one-sided.
★★See step 3 before cutting fabric.

Quilt Top Assembly
1. Join 2 pink pieces (A) 3 times for centers of tulips, as shown in Block Piecing Diagram I. Join a dark pink piece (A) to opposite sides of tulip

2. Alternate tulip blocks with 11½″ squares and triangles (O, P) in diagonal rows, as shown in Setting Diagram and quilt photograph. (Note the positions of the tulip blocks in quilt photograph and

Setting Diagram.) Join to form rows. Join rows and corner triangles (P).

3. Cut 4 borders, 6½" wide, from muslin. Join to quilt and miter corners.

Quilting

Outline-quilt ¼" inside seam lines of all pieces, except stems, in tulip block. Outline-quilt outside seam lines of stems. Quilt a feathered wreath in each 11" square and a half-wreath in triangles O and P. Refer to quilt photograph for position of plumes along the borders before quilting them.

Finished Edges

Bind with muslin.

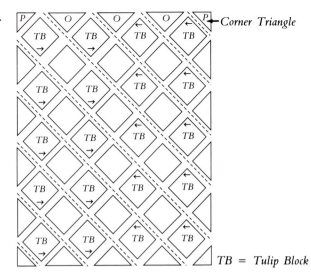

Setting Diagram

TB = *Tulip Block*

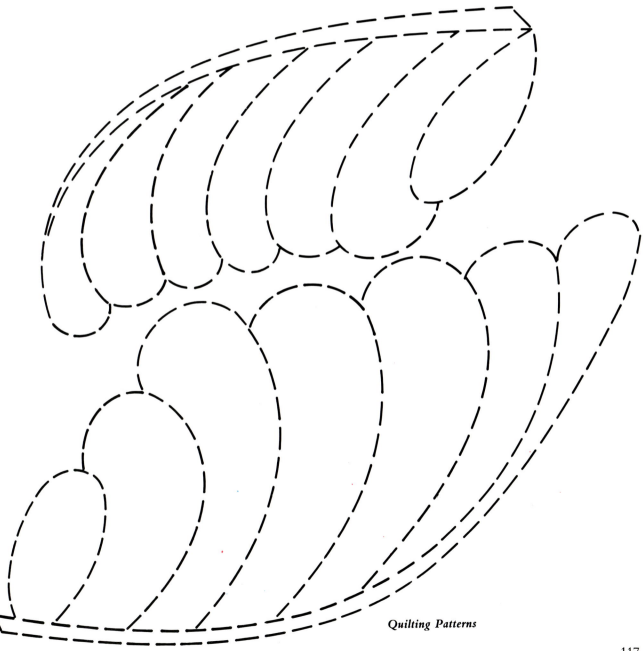

Quilting Patterns

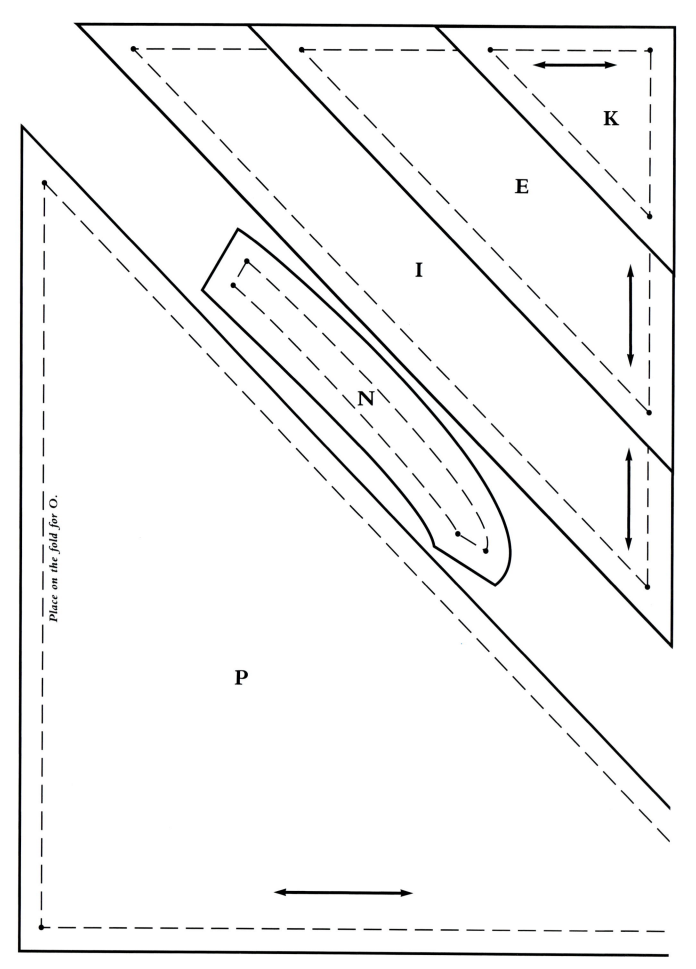

K

E

I

N

P

Place on the fold for O.

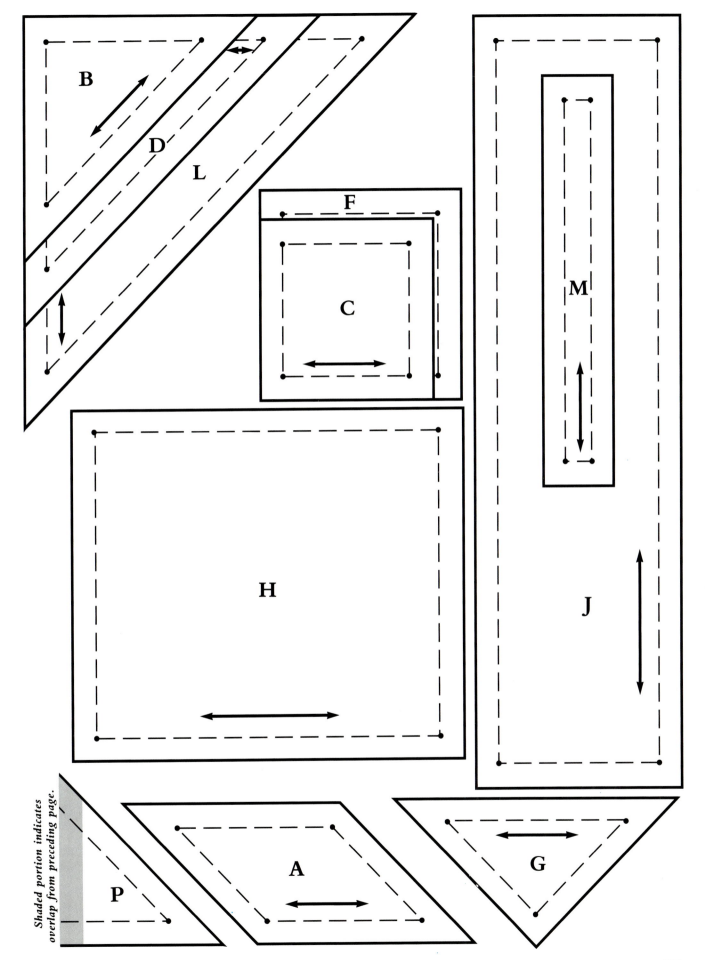

B

D

L

F

C

M

H

J

Shaded portion indicates
overlap from preceding page.

P

A

G

119

Mary Eleanor Keller (far left),
Mary Elizabeth Brading (standing),
Nancy Keller, and Jennifer C. Rozens

Mary Eleanor Keller, Mary Elizabeth Brading, Nancy Keller & Jennifer C. Rozens

Arrowsmith, Illinois, and Detroit, Michigan

On a farm outside the small town of Arrowsmith, Illinois, around the middle of the last century, three ladies found that the necessity of making quilts filled their evenings. Old shirts, dresses, and such were gathered for cutting patchwork pieces, and by lamplight the ladies pieced and quilted until bedtime. Mary Eleanor Keller and her two daughters, Mary Elizabeth and Nancy, spent their daytime hours doing farm chores. But we suspect that they welcomed each sunset, because it meant that they could lay down their tools, pick up their needles, relax, and enjoy an evening of quilting together.

We can only speculate on all of this, but the box of quilt blocks they left behind seems to affirm it. Jennifer Rozens, Mary Eleanor's great-granddaughter, inherited this box. She thought it contained only fabric scraps, but she found, instead, that it held 127 Evening Star blocks, 51 Double Wedding Ring arches, and 48 Double-T blocks, plus assorted scraps. Jennifer has thus far made two quilts from the blocks. "These quilts are my family," says Jennifer, "my history, and my reason for being proud to be a quilter."

Evening Star
Blocks pieced 1860s
Quilt set and quilted 1989
A quartet of quilters and a span of four generations are represented in *Evening Star.* A little more than two years ago, Jennifer Rozens decided she wanted to learn to quilt and remembered the little box of her great-grandmother's scraps stored in her mom's attic. When she opened the box, she found, to her surprise and delight, that the box contained, not scraps as she had thought, but dozens and dozens of quilt blocks.

As her introduction to quiltmaking, Jennifer chose the Evening Star blocks in the box. Never having made a quilt, she carefully hand-pieced and hand-quilted *Evening Star.* "And to think my mom trusted me with these blocks!" exclaims Jennifer.

Jennifer documented the quilt's history with a long poem, typed on fabric and appliquéd to the back of the quilt. In it she speaks to her ancestors:

"I hope you all forgive the size of my stitches,
On my second quilt I learned to stitch in the ditches!
I cry when I think that I put your stars together,
But I thank you all for making me a quilter forever and ever."

Evening Star

Finished Quilt Size
56" x 65"

Number of Blocks and Finished Size
120 blocks—4½" x 4½"

Fabric Requirements
Plaids   —2 yd.
Muslin   —2½ yd.
Navy   —1¾ yd.
Pink for bias
  binding   —1 yd.
Backing   —4 yd.

Number to Cut
Template A   —120 plaids
Template B   —960 plaids
                  480 muslin
Template C   —480 muslin

Quilt Top Assembly
1. Join triangles (B) to squares (A and C), as shown in Block Piecing Diagram. Make 120 blocks.

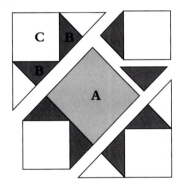

Block Piecing Diagram

2. Join blocks at sides in 12 rows of 10 blocks each. (See quilt photograph.) Join rows.
3. Cut 2 borders, 6" wide, from navy. Join to opposite sides of quilt. Cut 2 borders, 6" wide, from navy. Join to top and bottom of quilt.

Quilting
Quilt patchwork area in a 1" cross-hatching pattern. The navy border is quilted with an unbroken cable.

Finished Edges
Bind with pink fabric.

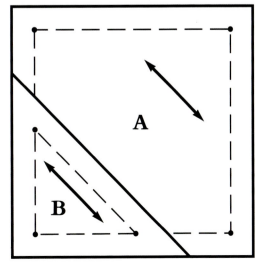

BEE
QUILTERS

The Rather Bees of Grand Island, Nebraska

The Australian Connection of New South Wales, Australia

International Quilting Bee
Grand Island, Nebraska

The Peacock Quilters of Devon, England

"My Quilting Guild of the Mailbox!" That's what Rita Hays of Grand Island, Nebraska, likes to call this international quilting group. Rita started corresponding with quilters in other states and countries more than four years ago. "We have a very active relationship," says Rita, "trading fabrics, books, ideas, and quilt blocks." The trading and correspondence took a more productive turn when three groups across the oceans (Pacific and Atlantic) decided to make quilts together without ever leaving home!

Rita's group, the Rather Bees, along with Dale Ritson and her group, The Australian Connection, of New South Wales, Australia, and Jane Syers and her group, The Peacock Quilters, of Devon, England, traded quilt blocks and fabrics as part of an international challenge. Each of the 21 participating quilters swapped four 12-inch Ohio Star blocks and a sample of sashing fabric with a member of a group in another country. All were challenged to make a quilt with the blocks and fabrics they received. Each quilter made any needed additional blocks, striving to maintain a continuity of colors and designs with the blocks she received.

"Twenty-one quilts were made this way," says Rita. "What a thrill it was for us to receive the slides of the finished quilts!" As a bonus, many lasting friendships were made. The monthly meeting of the Rather Bees always includes updates from one member or another about her pen pal and their projects. Photos and fabrics pass regularly across the Atlantic and Pacific oceans.

International Ohio Star
1990

The *International Ohio Star* is one of 21 quilts made as a part of an international quilt challenge. (See story above.) The quilt was designed and quilted by Rita Hays of Grand Island, Nebraska, with blocks made by Lea Lane of Hornsby, New South Wales, Australia, and Julie Shaw of Exeter, Devon, England.

The Ohio Star pattern was chosen for the challenge because it is readily recognizable around the world. Rita used partial seaming techniques to make stars in her sashing rows with fewer seams. (See steps 2 and 5 in instructions.)

Says Rita, "It is a little harder to piece this way, but there are no seams in the star center to quilt over."

"When this project began," she says, "these ladies were unknown quilters to me, half a world away. Now, they have become my best friends."

International Ohio Star

Finished Quilt Size
70″ x 86″ (without prairie points)

Number of Blocks and Finished Size
12 blocks—12″ x 12″

Fabric Requirements

Muslin	—1⅞ yd.
Lt. blue print	—2½ yd.
Sashing print	—3¼ yd.
Scrap prints	—2½ yd. total
Backing	—5 yd.

Number to Cut

Template A	—56 muslin
	4 scrap prints
	4 sashing print★
Template B	—48 muslin
	160 lt. blue print★
	18 sashing print★
	144 scrap prints★★
Template C	—31 sashing print★
Template D	—20 muslin
3″ square	—212 scrap prints

★See steps 6 and 7 before cutting fabrics.
★★Cut triangles in 12 fabric sets of 4 and 12 fabric sets of 8.

Quilt Top Assembly
1. Join squares (A) and triangles (B), as shown in Block Piecing Diagram. Make 4 blocks with scrap print centers and 8 blocks with muslin centers. (Arrange fabric sets for best color combinations before making blocks.)

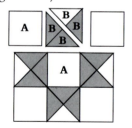

Block Piecing Diagram

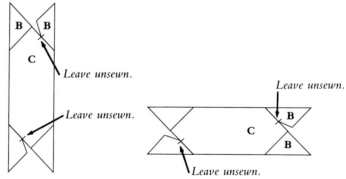

Vertical and Horizontal Sashing Piecing Diagrams

2. To make sashing, join 4 lt. blue print triangles (B) to piece C, as shown in Vertical and Horizontal Sashing Piecing Diagrams. Sew partial seams as shown. Partial seams are necessary for the insertion of square (D). (See step 5.) Make 16 vertical sashing sections and 15 horizontal sashing sections.

3. Cut 14 sashing rectangles, 4½″ x 12½″, from sashing print.
   Arrange blocks in 4 rows of 3 blocks each in best color combination. Arrange 2 sashing rectangles, 4 vertical sashing sections, and 3 blocks, as shown in Row Assembly Diagram, and join. Make 4 rows.

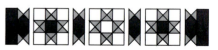

Row Assembly Diagram

4. Join horizontal sashing sections to rows, as shown in Setting Diagram.

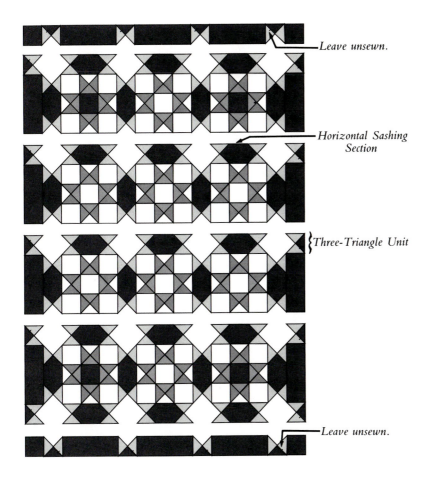

Leave unsewn.

Horizontal Sashing Section

Three-Triangle Unit

Leave unsewn.

Setting Diagram

Make 18 three-triangle units, using 2 lt. blue print triangles and 1 sashing print triangle for each unit, as shown in Setting Diagram. When making units, leave a portion of seam unsewn, as shown. Join a unit (2 in row 4) to sashing rectangle found at each end of each row, as shown. Arrange the remaining 8 units with sashing rectangles and squares (A) to form top and bottom sashing rows, as shown in Setting Diagram.

Join rows, leaving vacant areas for insertion of squares (D).

5. Join square (D) to opposite sides of sashing sections (seam 1 and seam 2), as shown in Sashing Square Insertion Diagram I. Then sew square to remaining sides, beginning each seam where partial sashing seam ended, as shown in Sashing Square Insertion Diagram II.

6. Cut 4 border strips, 1½″ wide, from lt. blue print. Join to quilt and miter corners.

7. Cut 4 borders, 4½″ wide, from sashing print. Join to quilt and miter corners.

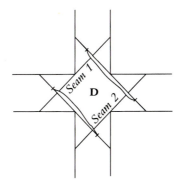

Sashing Square Insertion Diagram I

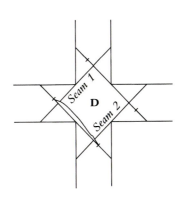

Sashing Square Insertion Diagram II

Quilting

Outline-quilt outside seam lines of Ohio Star pieces, sashing sections, and border strip. Quilt geometric pattern in each square D. Borders are quilted in an unbroken diamond pattern. Blue quilting thread is used.

Finished Edges

For prairie points, fold each 3″ square as shown in Prairie Point Folding Diagram. Arrange prairie points in a continuous, overlapping fashion for sides, top, and bottom, as shown in Prairie Point Arrangement Diagram. (Overlap 58 points for each side, and 48 each for the top and bottom.) Baste prairie points together.

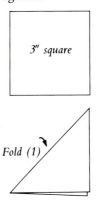

3″ square

Fold (1)

Fold (2)

Prairie Point Folding Diagrams

Prairie Point Arrangement Diagram

With raw edges together, stitch prairie points to quilt top, as shown in Prairie Point Attachment Diagrams. Turn under raw edge of quilt back to cover raw edges of prairie points and blindstitch in place.

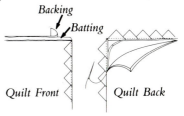

Backing

Batting

Quilt Front

Quilt Back

Prairie Point Attachment Diagrams

Quilt Documentation
Prairie points are repeated on the back of the quilt to enhance the quilt documentation. (See photograph.)

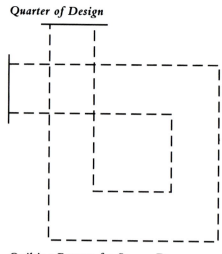

Quilting Pattern for Square D

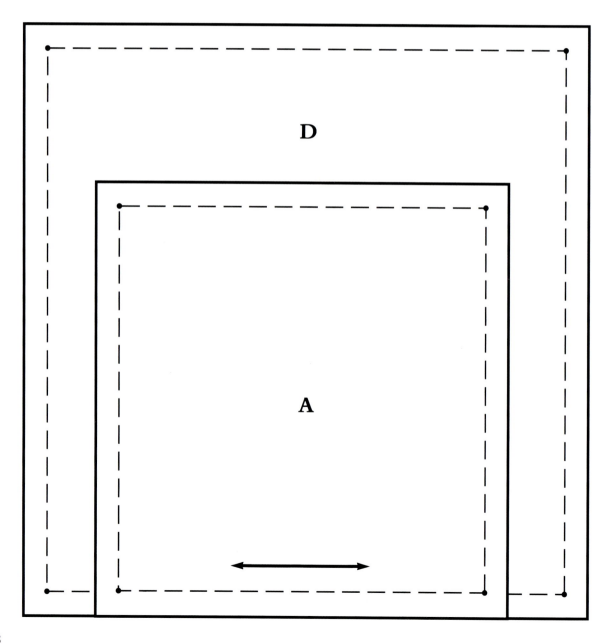

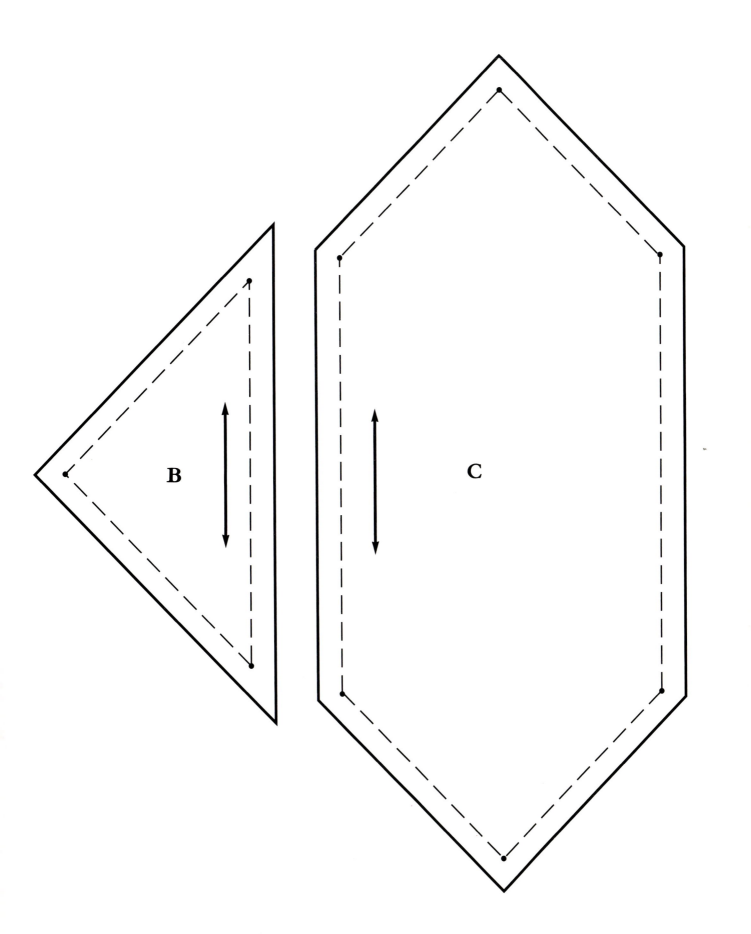

B

C

Gathering for their bi-monthly meeting are Chippewa County Piecemakers: (seated, left to right) Betty Hutson, Marky Kuba, Phyllis Vetterkind, and Sue Sorum, and (standing, left to right) Judy Gaier, Joyce Sperber, Margaret Schoenberg, Margaret Spaeth, Shorty Vodacek, and Rose Zimmerman.

Chippewa County Piecemakers

Chippewa Falls, Wisconsin

Seven years ago several of the founding members of what is now the Chippewa County Piecemakers were taking quilting classes offered by the local vocational school. As the time approached for the classes to end, they realized that they were disappointed that their time together would soon be over. They began asking around to see who would be interested in continuing to meet, and shortly thereafter the Chippewa County Piecemakers was founded.

The group continues to thrive and grow today. Anyone is welcome to join, and new members often hear of the Piecemakers through ads the group runs in the newspaper and on the local television station. Meetings are held twice a month, and once a year the group combines talents and creates a community service project quilt, such as the one presented below.

Hearts of Chippewa
1990

What more appropriate place to hang a quilt with hearts than in a cardiac rehabilitation center? No one can count the number of patients who must have felt a sense of caring and kindness from the presence of this quilt in the cardiac exercise and monitoring room. The quilt has since been raffled by the hospital and the Chippewa County Piecemakers. They are proud to say that enough money was raised to purchase a piece of exercise equipment for the center.

This quilt is made from a traditional pattern that is designed to catch the eye and awake the viewer to the secondary pattern of stars. "Once you have spotted a star, your eye keeps searching for another," says Marky Kuba, one of the project coordinators. All of the Chippewa County Piecemakers contributed to the making of this quilt. They are Muriel Boyken, Agatha Dachel, Judy Gaier, Betty Hutson, Marky Kuba, Margaret Schoenberg, Sue Sorum, Margaret Spaeth, Joyce Sperber, Phyllis Vetterkind, Shorty Vodacek, and Rose Zimmerman.

heart to aid in the positioning of fabric heart. Glue fabric heart to muslin, using glue sparingly along heart edges. Appliqué heart.

Cut muslin from behind each heart, leaving ¼″ seam allowance. Soak each square in cool water for 15 to 20 seconds to loosen and dissolve glue. Lift out freezer paper heart. Blot excess water from square by rolling it in a towel. Press with a dry iron.

3. Alternate dark hearts with medium hearts and arrange squares in 9 rows of 7 squares each. (The Chippewa Piecemakers suggest laying out squares on the floor.)

Begin to "deal out" triangles to form a star around each heart, as shown in Setting Diagram and photograph. (Area within bold-lined square indicates how a star is formed with the triangles.) A dark heart will take a dark star, and a medium heart will take a medium star. (You will have triangles left over. The Chippewa Piecemakers felt that it was easier to cut 8 triangles from each fabric because you don't know which fabrics will be used until the hearts are made and arranged. Add the excess triangles to your scrap bag for your next project.)

Setting Diagram

Once completed, survey your arrangement and shift star sets if necessary. Try to keep colors evenly distributed to avoid clumps of color and to help each star show up distinctly.

4. Before stitching triangles to squares, tag each heart square with a block and row number to maintain proper order. Stitch triangles to corners of squares.

5. Join blocks at sides to form rows. Join rows.

6. Cut 2 borders, 6½″ wide, from blue print and join to top and bottom of quilt.

Hearts of Chippewa

Finished Quilt Size
82″ x 102″

Number of Blocks and Finished Size
63 blocks—10″ x 10″

Fabric Requirements
Scraps★ — 6⅝ yd. total
Muslin — 5 yd.
Blue print — 3 yd.
Blue for
   bias binding — 1 yd.
Backing — 6 yd.

★For triangles, a strip approximately 6″ x 24″ is needed from each of 26 dark fabrics and 24 medium fabrics. For hearts, a 6½″ square is needed from each of 32 dark fabrics and 31 medium fabrics.

Other Materials
Freezer paper
Fabric-compatible glue stick

Number to Cut
Triangle — 400 scraps★★
★★Cut 8 triangles from each of 50 different fabrics. See step 3.

Quilt Top Assembly
1. Cut sixty-three 7½″ squares from muslin. Cut sixty-three 6½″ squares from heart fabrics. (Cut 1 square per fabric.) Trace 63 hearts without seam allowance on dull side of freezer paper. Cut out hearts on traced lines. Press hearts, shiny side down, to wrong side of 6½″ squares. Cut out, adding ¼″ seam allowance.

On wrong side of fabric, run a line of glue along the seam allowance. With your thumb, carefully pinch-roll the seam allowance to the back (freezer paper), holding the fabric in position long enough for the glue to take hold. Keep curves smooth.

2. Position heart pattern on each muslin square and lightly trace

7. Cut 2 borders, 6½″ wide, from blue print and join to sides of quilt.

Quilting
Quilt in-the-ditch around each heart and outline-quilt ¼″ outside heart seam line. Quilt in-the-ditch of muslin and triangle seam lines. Outline-quilt ¼″ inside and outside triangle seam lines.

For blocks contiguous to side borders, quilt "missing" star points (triangles) at ends of alternating rows, beginning with row 2. (See Quilting Diagram.) Quilt remainder of border with hearts, as shown.

Quilting Diagram

Finished Edges
Trim border for round corners, as shown on quilt photograph. Bind quilt with a double-French fold bias binding from blue fabric.

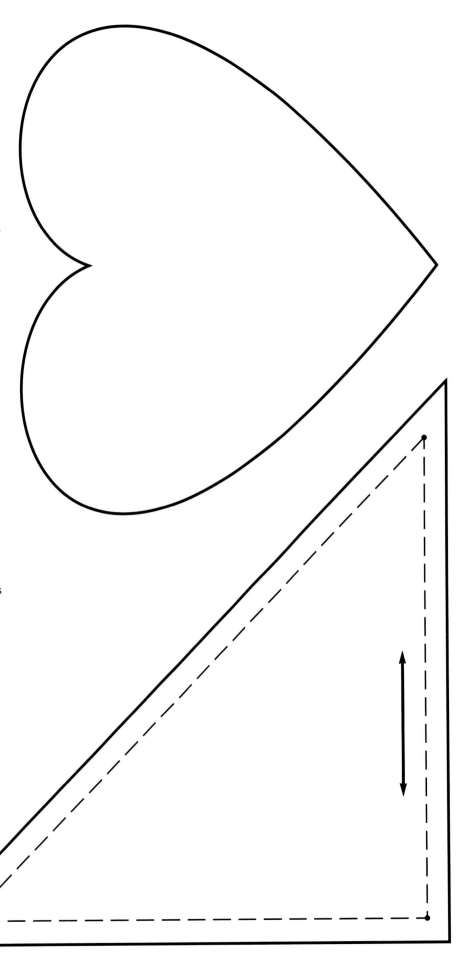

Piecemakers

Mechanicsville, Virginia

The Piecemakers is one of seven chapters that make up the Richmond Quilting Guild of Richmond, Virginia. The large membership and the diversity of schedules among the guild caused members to naturally gravitate into smaller groups with more accommodating meeting times and locations. This format was so successful that these smaller groups later became organized chapters.

The Piecemakers was the fifth chapter to be organized, and the majority of its members are from Mechanicsville, a city seven miles northeast of Richmond. The group meets formally once a month, but this just simply isn't enough for these quilting enthusiasts. "We have a small quilting bee that meets every Monday afternoon at the local library," says Beverley Cosby, an active member of the chapter. "It's great fun because the library has loaned us a large work area where we can quilt and a place for storage of our projects. We can work on a chapter project, each other's quilts, our own, or just talk and enjoy ourselves. It's a great complement to our regular monthly chapter meetings."

Hanover Tulip
1990
The simplicity and symmetry of this lovely quilt will invite you to make more than one. At least, that has been the case with the Piecemakers. Members are in the process of completing a total of six *Hanover Tulip* quilts in a variety of colors for themselves and others.

The first quilt, which you see here, was made for the Richmond Quilting Guild's quilt exhibit. Every chapter is responsible for making one raffle quilt to raise funds for the exhibit. Beverley Cosby was asked to design the Piecemakers' quilt. She was inspired by a block she had seen with four appliquéd hearts. "I began with the simple heart shape and added the bud at the top and a stem and leaves," says Beverley, "and it became a tulip."

All of the members were very pleased with Beverley's design since it was one that quilters at any level of experience could make with little difficulty. Hanover is the name of the county where all of the Piecemakers live.

The makers of *Hanover Tulip* are Karen Arbaugh, Virginia Beck, Gladys Bragg, Beverley Cosby, Lois Dotson, Lillian Earhart, Fran Edmonds, Edith Fensome, Ruby Habron, Geneva Herod, Lurlean Jackson, Margaret Jenkins, Bernice Kerr, Lillie Lee, Debra Lusk, Brownie Mosher, Berchie Oakley, Dorothy Parrish, Phyllis Snead, Lareve Waleski, Gertrude Walker, and Catherine Young.

Hanover Tulip

Finished Quilt Size
82¼" x 97¾"

Number of Blocks and Finished Size
20 Tulip blocks—11" x 11"

Fabric Requirements
Green print   —2 yd.
Maroon print   —3 yd.
Pink print   —1⅝ yd.
Muslin   —6 yd.
Green print for
  bias binding   —1¼ yd.
Backing   —5¾ yd.

Other Materials
Freezer paper
Fabric-compatible glue stick
  (optional)

Number to Cut
Template A★   —40 green print
Template B★   —124 green print
Template C★   —102 pink print
Template D★   —102 maroon
            print★★
Template E   —14 pink print
Template F   —4 pink print
★See step 2 before cutting fabric.
★★See steps 4 and 6 before cutting fabric.

Quilt Top Assembly
1. Cut thirty-two 11½" squares from muslin. (See step 5 before cutting muslin.) Set aside 12. Finger-crease remaining 20 squares on the diagonal; then finger-crease again on the opposite diagonal to form guidelines for appliqué. Finger-crease the squares in half twice for additional guidelines.
2. Trace pattern pieces A through D without seam allowance on dull side of freezer paper. Make number of each piece listed above and mark grain line arrows and any placement lines on each piece. Cut out pieces on traced lines. Press pieces, shiny side down, on wrong side of fabric. Cut fabric, adding ¼" seam allowance. Turn seam allowance to back of paper and baste the seam allowance over the edge of the freezer paper. (Some quilters may prefer to stick down the seam allowance with fabric glue.)
  Arrange pieces on muslin square, as shown in Placement Diagram. Layer-appliqué pieces in place.

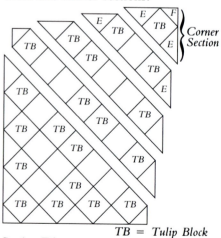

(Numbers in parentheses in Placement Diagram indicate the order for appliquéing.) Appliqué both stems (A) before leaves (B), and buds (C) before hearts (D). Appliqué 20 tulip blocks. Cut out fabric from behind pieces, leaving ¼" seam allowance, and remove freezer paper.

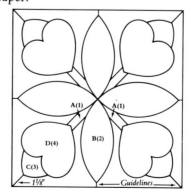

Placement Diagram

3. Arrange tulip blocks with muslin squares and triangles (E) in diagonal

rows and corner sections, as shown in Setting Diagram, and join. Join rows and corner sections.

TB = *Tulip Block*

Setting Diagram

4. Cut 4 borders, 1½" wide, from maroon print. Join borders to quilt and miter corners.
5. Cut 4 borders, 8½" wide, from muslin. Join to quilt and miter

136

corners. Arrange single tulips on borders, as shown in quilt photograph, being sure to align side border tulips opposite the tulips in blocks in a mirror-image fashion. Layer-appliqué tulips to border.
6. Cut 4 borders, 1½″ wide, from maroon print. Join to quilt and miter corners.

Quilting
Outline-quilt outside seam lines of all appliquéd pieces. Outline-quilt inside seam lines of muslin squares. Feather wreaths are quilted in each plain muslin square and plumes in each pink print triangle. Diagonal lines of quilting, ¾″ apart, are background-quilted on the muslin border.

Finished Edges
Bind with green print fabric.

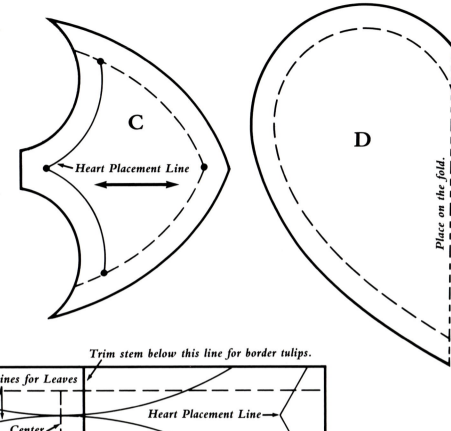

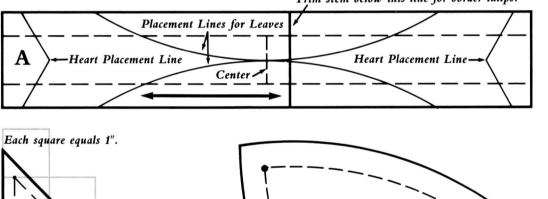

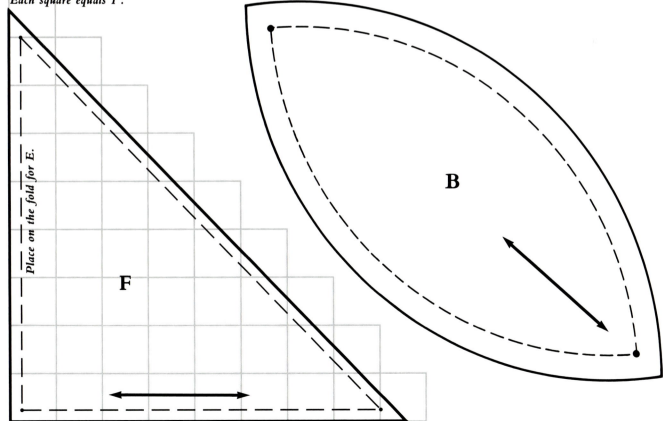

DESIGNER
GALLERY

Six members of the Mountain Maverick Quilters are (seated, left to right)—Mary Ann Schmidt, Nancy Grove, Barbara Caves, and (standing, left to right)—Flo Cox, Susan Ennis, and Wanda Pettersen.

Mountain Maverick Quilters

Morrison, Colorado

The leader of the Mountain Maverick Quilters, Mary Ann Schmidt, says that their group's purpose is not only to make quilts, but also to give each other moral support. Formed in 1989, Mountain Maverick Quilters is composed of ten individuals of varied interests. The topics of discussion at their weekly meetings range from world events and books to gourmet food preparation and wines, in addition to quilting.

As a group, they attend quilt shows, visit fabric shops, and occasionally prepare a gourmet dinner. Original quilt designs, such as the one below, are their specialty. Their second group quilt, named *Zillions of Diamonds*, is in the works and uses hundreds of fabrics, each carefully hand-dyed to just the right shade.

Sierra Blanca
1989

Towering above the forests of southern Colorado stands Blanca Peak, the highest peak in the Sangre de Cristo mountains. Love for this spectacular Colorado scenery and for quilting inspired the Mountain Maverick Quilters to make *Sierra Blanca*.

A line drawing of Blanca Peak, prepared by one of their members, was projected onto a sheet of paper with 3½"-wide parallel lines drawn from top to bottom. Pattern shapes and sizes were determined, marked between the parallel lines (called channels), and numbered. Then members made corresponding muslin channels with pattern lines. Fabrics were stitched to channels, starting from the tree trunks and working upward. "We worked on one channel at a time," says Mary Ann Schmidt, "selecting fabrics as we went along to come as close to nature as possible." One whole day was spent dyeing fabric to just the perfect shade of blue to duplicate the gorgeous Colorado sky. Members of the Mountain Maverick Quilters who participated in the making of *Sierra Blanca* were: Flo Cox, Susan Ennis, Nancy Grove, Joyce Horne, Nancy Roth, Mary Ann Schmidt, and Jane Steele.

Sara Ann McLennand

Wellington, Florida

Almost five years ago, Sara Ann was inspired by a quilt competition to venture into the world of original quilt designing. "Before that," she says, "I used traditional patterns in order to understand technique and workmanship. Now my quilts are almost solely original designs." This break from traditional patterns and the national recognition that she received for her quilts have given her the confidence to continue. Her most recent quilt, *Reaching for the Moon*, was one of two quilts from Florida accepted for the national touring exhibit of the Discover America Quilt Show.

Sara Ann is a member of the Palm Beach County Quilter's Guild and is past coordinator of their annual show, which is the largest professionally judged quilt show in Florida.

Coiled Symmetry
1989

Coiled Symmetry is Sara Ann's second in a series of three quilts based upon flat Indian basket designs. Sara Ann summoned her skills and training in the arts and in textile weaving to transform three-dimensional designs into colorful flat ones for her series. Each quilt is made entirely of chintz. "Although chintz is more difficult to quilt," explains Sara Ann, "it adds dimension to the quilt with its subtle sheen and rich color."

To achieve accuracy in piecing and grain line direction, Sara Ann drafts the entire quilt on freezer paper. (That's 80 inches by 80 inches, quilters!) Pieces are cut from the quilt drawing so that every piece has its own pattern.

Coiled Symmetry has won several ribbons and appears in *Quilt Art '91 Engagement Calendar*, published by the American Quilter's Society. (See "Resources.") Enjoy seeing and making Sara Ann's first quilt in her basket series, *Duck Island Basket*, in "The Basket Patch" chapter.

Carolyn Mazloomi

Cincinnati, Ohio

Carolyn Mazloomi is particularly interested in reviving and maintaining the art of quilting among black people. "I know that our grandmothers and great-grandmothers quilted, but as I traveled to quilt shows, I rarely saw any black quilters," she says. Motivated by her determination to organize these quilters, she placed an ad in a major quilt publication in 1983, asking black quilters to write to her. As a result, she founded the Women of Color Quilters Network. Says Carolyn, "Today, we have more than 300 quilters in the network—from across the United States as well as in Jamaica, Russia, Europe, South America, and Australia." She explains that the goals of the group are to keep quilting alive within the black community and to get young black people interested in quilting.

There's Unity in Family
1990

Hands reaching out to help or caress; faces of fathers, mothers, and children; symbols of home, church, and school—these are the components of *There's Unity in Family*, Carolyn's salute to the family. "The family was once a very close-knit unit," she says, "and I hope it will be once again. I don't think people value family as much as in past decades."

This wall hanging is Carolyn's original design, hand-painted with fabric paint on chintz. The piecework is machine-appliquéd to the surface with wide zigzag stitching.

There's Unity in Family has been exhibited at the Cincinnati Museum of Natural History and Tangeman Fine Arts Gallery, both in Cincinnati, Ohio; National Afro-American Museum in Wilberforce, Ohio; Heritage Center, North Carolina A & T State University in Greensboro, North Carolina; Troy-Hayner Cultural Center in Troy, Ohio; and at the Louisville Museum of History and Science in Louisville, Kentucky.

Erika Carter
Bellevue, Washington

Within two years of making her first quilt, Erika was a blue ribbon winner. Since then, her quiltmaking accomplishments have taken off. Her quilts have been displayed in exhibitions, both nationally and internationally. In 1991, she conducted her second solo quilt exhibition, which was held in Stockholm, Sweden, at the Galleri Bennetter. Her quilts were also a part of Quilt National '91, a traveling exhibition in the United States.

The majority of her quilts are wall hangings, inspired by her desire to reproduce the beauty of nature in fabric form. Strip-pieced wall hangings using a multitude of prints have become her trademark. "This method best explores my interest in texture," says Erika. "I love fabric, color, patterns, textures, and the padded feeling of a quilt. In quilting, I have found my creative medium."

Reverence
1989
Shimmering flashes of color flit before our eyes as the rushing breezes of fall sweep leaves from their moorings. We are so awestruck by the cyclical beauty of nature that in its presence we are often speechless. Erika's *Reverence* reminds us of those days when nature freely gives us a spectacle of color to lift our spirits.

Painstakingly, Erika positioned every leaf and branch on her strip-pieced background and hand-appliquéd them in place. "I design all my quilts on the dining room wall," she says. "But I also enjoy the hand quilting because it gives me time to reflect on the piece and to develop new ideas."

Timberline II
1991
If you have ever been snow skiing or backpacking in the mountains of our scenic West, then you are probably familiar with the view from just above the timberline. As you look down through the trees, the sky is a myriad of blues, interrupted by the angular contours of that last stand of weather-tested trees.

Living in Washington, Erika is only a few hours away from a timberline view. But the rest of us need someone like Erika to bring the view to us. Her handling of fabric colors requires skill, patience, and an allegiance to detail. Her quilts not only portray an image of nature but evoke the essence of it.

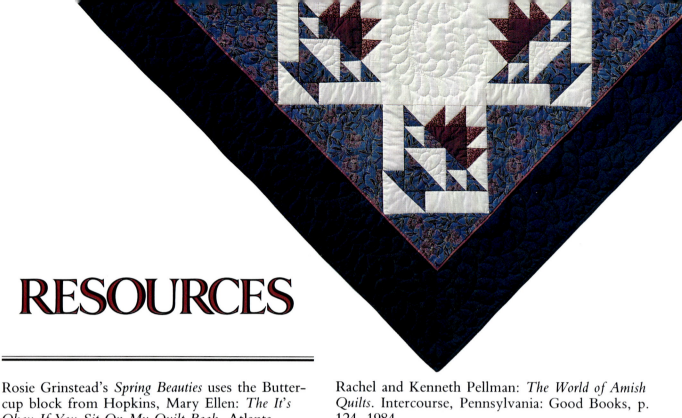

RESOURCES

Rosie Grinstead's *Spring Beauties* uses the Buttercup block from Hopkins, Mary Ellen: *The It's Okay If You Sit On My Quilt Book*. Atlanta, Georgia: Yours Truly, Inc., p. 61, 1982.

Sandra Gould's design for *Whirligig in a Summer Breeze* was inspired by the Pinwheel block, which originally appeared in Hinson DA: *Quilting Manual*. New York: Hearthside Press, 1966.

Joe's Quilt, made by Karen Buckley, was an adaptation of *Morning Glory Lane* found in *Quiltmaker*, 8:34 and 46, 1989.

Marta Amundson was inspired by an Amish quilt, *King's Cross Variation*, c. 1930, found in

Rachel and Kenneth Pellman: *The World of Amish Quilts*. Intercourse, Pennsylvania: Good Books, p. 124, 1984.

The hibiscus pattern used by Linda Lewis can be found in Root, Elizabeth: *Hawaiian Quilting*. New York: Dover Publications, Inc., p. 21, 1989.

Beverley Cosby's *Frank's Star* appeared in *'90 American Quilter's Society Calendar*. Paducah, Kentucky: American Quilter's Society, 1990.

Sara Ann McLennand's *Coiled Symmetry* appeared in *Quilt Art '91 Engagement Calendar*. Paducah, Kentucky: American Quilter's Society, 1990.